DTS-34-FA65-LR1
DTS-34-FP01-LR1

Study of Visitor Response to Air Tour and Other Aircraft Noise in National Parks

Amanda S. Rapoza

Gregg G Fleming

Cynthia S.Y. Lee

Christopher J. Roof

U.S. Department of Transportation

Research and Special Programs Administration

John A. Volpe National Transportation Systems Center

Environmental Measurement and Modeling Division, DTS-34

Acoustics Facility

Kendall Square

Cambridge, MA 02142

January 2005

U.S. Department of Transportation

Federal Aviation Administration

TABLE OF CONTENTS

LIST OF FIGURES

Environmental Measurement and Modeling Division
Volpe Center Acoustics Facility   January 2005
Study of Visitor Response to Air Tour and Other Aircraft Noise in National Parks

LIST OF TABLES

EXECUTIVE SUMMARY

This document summarizes the findings of a study that considers all known aircraft noise dose and visitor response data previously collected in the National Parks. These data consist of almost 2500 visitor interviews and simultaneous acoustical measurements collected at four different National Parks between 1992 and 1999. These data are used to develop relationships that relate the noise (dose) data to visitor response for assessing aircraft noise in the National Parks.

In addition to the development of dose-response relationships, the study focused several key questions. The questions, followed by the conclusions that can be drawn from the results of this study, are as follows:

1. *Is visitor response to the 'annoyance' question different from visitor response to the 'interference' question (i.e., "Were you bothered or annoyed by aircraft noise during your visit to the site?" versus "How much did the sound from aircraft interfere with you enjoyment of the site?")?*

   No, the vast majority of visitors (92.4%-94.4%) rate annoyance equal to or higher than interference with enjoyment, signifying that the use of annoyance, if anything, provides for a more conservative assessment (i.e., with annoyance, visitors would expect to be impacted at lower levels as compared with interference with enjoyment).

2. *Should visitor response be dichotomized based on the top two of five steps on the response scale, the top three, or the top four?*

   No one dichotomization can be said to perform well in both statistical goodness-of-fit and reliability tests. Therefore, there is no definitive scientific evidence present to reliably choose a dichotomization. As a result, the dose-response curves are presented for response dichotomizations that use both the top three (as used in previous park visitor response studies) and the top two (as used in residential studies) dichotomizations.

3. *Is there any evidence that visitors are less annoyed by high altitude jet overflight noise than by tour aircraft overflight noise?*

   Visitors appear to be less sensitive to high-altitude jet overflight noise as compared with noise from tour aircraft. However, the data does not show this with statistical certainty and no definitive conclusions can be drawn. Consequently, all analyses presented herein treat aircraft noise in the aggregate (high altitude jets and air tours combined), recognizing that air tour noise is the dominant contributor to the overall aircraft sound level for the data included herein.

4. *Is visitor response to tour aircraft overflight noise similar for sites of the same type (i.e., overlook versus short hike sites) within the same park?*

   Yes, the following were proven to be similar:
   Bryce Canyon overlooks: Bryce Point, Rainbow Point, and Fairyland
   Grand Canyon SR overlooks: Pima Point and Lipan Point
   Grand Canyon NR overlooks: Point Imperial 1999 and Point Imperial 1992
   Bryce Canyon short hikes: Queens Garden and Queens Garden Extended

5. *Is visitor response to tour aircraft overflight noise similar for different parks?*

   Overlooks: It was found that while overlook sites at Bryce Canyon and Grand Canyon (NR) are statistically similar, there were differences between these sites and Grand Canyon (SR). Although the difference between these two groups of sites is statistically significant, it may not be a practical enough difference upon which to base separate dose-response curves, given the required added complexity.

   Short Hikes: Analysis showed that the short hike sites were found to be statistically similar at different parks and could be combined by limiting the respondents to those who completed the entire hike and by including first visit as a covariate.

6. *Is visitor response to tour aircraft overflight noise similar at different types of sites (i.e., overlook versus short hike) for different parks?*

   No, visitor response to tour aircraft overflight noise is not similar at overlooks and short hikes.

7. *Are there other factors, such as age or gender, which influence visitor response to tour aircraft overflight noise?*

   Yes, it appears that a respondent's familiarity with the site can influence visitor response to aircraft noise, i.e., repeat visitors generally are more annoyed.

8. *Does visitor response to tour aircraft overflight noise at the same location change over time?*

   No, an analysis of data from the Point Imperial overlook and Grand Canyon showed no significant difference in the relationship between acoustic dose and visitor response between the years 1992 and 1999. Because this type of analysis could only be performed for one study location, these results should be considered somewhat preliminary. At the same time, they do represent the best available information.

In addition, this document contains an example of how two noise descriptors could be combined for practical use in a National Park setting. It is believed that a combination will: 1) provide for a more complete assessment of visitor annoyance / interference with enjoyment; and 2) allow for the use of both a level-based acoustic descriptor, as well as an audibility-based descriptor. The acoustic descriptors are combined by determining their respective values on the dose-response relationship curves at equal levels of percent annoyance / interference with enjoyment. Graphics are presented which show %TAA and $\Delta L_{AE,Tac}$ values for equal annoyance levels in five percent increments. They show that it is possible to reduce annoyance by reducing either %TAA or $\Delta L_{AE,Tac}$.

Due to the underlying nature of the data used in this analysis, there are a number of items that should be considered before applying the dose-response relationships presented herein to other park environments.

- Ambient sound levels in the parks in this study ranged between 10 and 40 dBA. The appropriateness of applying these relationships to parks with ambient levels above about 40 dBA is not clear.
- The methodology presented herein only applies to the assessment of noise impact on park visitors. Special considerations will have to be given to wildlife and cultural impacts.
- The majority of the data underlying the short hike curves was measured at BCNP. This data consists, almost exclusively, of helicopter tours using a Bell 206L.
- There are underlying site biases that may influence the dose-response curves.

1.0 INTRODUCTION

This report presents the findings of a noise dose / visitor response study conducted by the Acoustics Facility at the United States Department of Transportation's John A. Volpe National Transportation Systems Center (U.S. DOT/Volpe Center). The primary tool used in the study is data relating quantitative noise dose and qualitative visitor response, or dose-response. This study considers all known aircraft noise dose-response data previously collected in the National Parks, a summary of which is presented in Section 1.1. The study focuses on the following key questions:

1. Is visitor response to the 'annoyance' question different from visitor response to the 'interference' question (i.e., "Were you bothered or annoyed by aircraft noise during your visit to the site?" versus "How much did the sound from aircraft interfere with your enjoyment of the site?")?
2. Should visitor response be dichotomized based on the top two of five steps on the response scale, the top three, or the top four?
3. Is there any evidence that visitors are less annoyed by high altitude jet overflight noise than by tour aircraft overflight noise?
4. Is visitor response to tour aircraft overflight noise similar for sites of the same type (i.e., overlook versus short hike sites) within the same park?
5. Is visitor response to tour aircraft overflight noise similar for different parks?
6. Is visitor response to tour aircraft overflight noise similar at different types of sites (i.e., overlook versus short hike) for different parks?
7. Are there other factors, such as age or gender, which influence visitor response to tour aircraft overflight noise?
8. Does visitor response to tour aircraft overflight noise at the same location change over time?

1.1 Data Sources

Data were obtained from two dose-response studies conducted jointly by the FAA and the Volpe Center,[1,2] and a third study conducted by the National Park Service (NPS) and the consulting firm, Harris, Miller, Miller, and Hanson (HMMH)[3]. Combined, the three studies include data from four National Parks for seven short hike sites and seven overlook sites. A short hike is generally defined as a site where visitors walk a distance along a well-marked trail to gain further enjoyment of a particular area. These hikes are generally less than 1 hour in duration and occur in frontcountry areas where there is substantial human activity. An overlook is generally defined as a frontcountry site where visitors can enjoy scenic vistas in close proximity to parking lots, visitor centers, etc. Table 1 summarizes the overlook sites at which data were obtained, along with the source of the data, the year the data were collected, and the number of surveys at that particular site. Table 2 presents similar information for short hike sites.

These three studies were conducted in a similar manner, remaining consistent in both acoustic measurement practices and survey techniques. The survey questionnaire was originally developed by HBRS, Inc. and circulated to the NPS, U.S. Forest Service, and a Technical Review Group consisting of experts selected by the NPS from the Department of Defense, the Federal Aviation Administration, universities, and public interest groups. This survey was then used for the NPS study detailed in Reference 3. The survey questionnaire was then appended (all questions in the original survey remained in tact, but some additional questions were added) for the FAA study in References 1 and 2. This modified survey instrument was reviewed and approved by the NPS as a condition to approving the research permit in each park.

Table 1. Overlook Dose-Response Data Sources

Park	Site	Source	Year	# Of Surveys
Bryce Canyon	Rainbow Point (RP)	Volpe[2]	1999	58
Bryce Canyon	Fairyland (FL)	Volpe[2]	1999	139
Bryce Canyon	Bryce Point (BP)	Volpe[2]	1999	43
Grand Canyon (NR)	Point Imperial (PI99)	Volpe[2]	1999	281
Grand Canyon (SR)	Pima Point (PP)	Volpe[2]	1999	162
Grand Canyon (SR)	Lipan Point (LP)	HMMH[3]	1992	183
Grand Canyon (NR)	Point Imperial (PI92)	HMMH[3]	1992	124

Table 2. Short Hike Dose-Response Data Sources

Park	Site	Source	Year	# Of Surveys
Bryce Canyon	Queens Garden Trail (QGT)	Volpe[1]	1998	514
Bryce Canyon	Queens Garden Trail Extended (QGTX)	Volpe[1]	1998	391
Haleakala	Sliding Sands Trail (SS)	HMMH[3]	1992	213
Hawaii Volcanoes	Wahahula Temple (WT)	HMMH[3]	1992	195
Grand Canyon (SR)*	Havasu Creek (HC)†	HMMH[3]	1992	30
Grand Canyon (SR)	Hermit Basin (HB)‡	HMMH[3]	1992	32
Grand Canyon (SR)	Pima Trail (PT)‡	Volpe[2]	1999	31

For overlooks, the current study initially included 990 cases with both uncontaminated acoustic data and respondent data. 52 respondents were not subjected to a noise dose; these cases were eliminated from the analysis. In addition, three respondents indicated that they had heard aircraft noise but failed to quantify their level of annoyance; these cases were also eliminated from the analysis. Eight respondents had a noise dose equal to zero, but indicated that they had heard aircraft noise during their visit; these cases were

---

* Although technically in the same park, the Grand Canyon overlook sites are on different sides of the Canyon, and represent a vastly different environment. Point Imperial is on the north rim (NR) of the Canyon, while both Pima Point and Lipan Point are on the south rim (SR) of the Canyon. Due to the sheer size of the Canyon, these sites are separated by large travel distances (typically six hours or more); consequentially visitors often do not visit both areas in the same trip. In fact, many visitors only have the opportunity to visit the south rim. Consequently, it is possible that there are fundamental differences in visitor expectations between the north and south rims. As a result, it was decided that these areas should initially be treated as separate parks (Grand Canyon (NR) and Grand Canyon (SR)).

† Data were not used because background sound levels (produced by waterfalls) were loud enough to prevent visitors from hearing aircraft and to prevent accurate measurements of the aircraft3.

‡ These sites were eliminated from the analysis due to: 1.) site type uncertainty, 2.) the limited number of surveys, and 3.) the limited range of aircraft noise dose observed at these sites. Appendix A contains further explanation.

not eliminated. In total, 935 cases remained for dose-response analysis: 209 from BCNP and 726 from GCNP.

In comparison, the short hike study initially included 1313 cases with both uncontaminated acoustic data and respondent data. Fifteen respondents were not subjected to a noise dose; these cases were eliminated from the analysis. In addition, 126 respondents indicated that they had heard aircraft noise but failed to quantify their level of annoyance; these cases were also eliminated from the analysis. Four respondents had a noise dose equal to zero, but indicated that they had heard aircraft noise during their visit; these cases were not eliminated. In total, 1172 cases remained for dose-response analysis: 779 from BCNP, 202 from Haleakala, and 191 from Hawaii Volcanoes.

1.1.1 General Overview of Data

Table 3 contains some general comparisons of visitor response.

Table 3 Overview of Responses

Percentage of Respondents who:	Overlook	Short Hike
Were exposed to noise dose >0	94%	89%
Reported hearing aircraft when noise dose >0	37%	66%
Reported moderate to extreme annoyance when noise dose >0	9%	26%
Reported very or extreme annoyance when noise dose >0	2%	12%

In comparing the respondents at overlooks to short hikes, a substantial difference exists in the percentage that report hearing aircraft when they are present, 37% to 66%, respectively. Although this observation is somewhat intuitive, it seems to indicate that overlook visitors are less sensitive to aircraft noise as compared to visitors on a short hike.

1.2 Data Processing

Raw dose-response data from HMMH were obtained and processed by the Volpe Center using the identical methodology as used for the Volpe data. For more information on the data reduction process, readers are directed to References 1 and 2. Section 1.2.1 describes the acoustic descriptors used, while Section 1.2.2 describes the dichotomization of the visitor response data.

1.2.1 Acoustic Dose

Visitor responses were related to the acoustic dose by means of 12 different acoustic descriptors. The acoustic descriptors are as follows:

> **Time-Based Descriptors**: 1) percentage time audible (%TA); 2) percentage time noticeable (%TN); 3) time above ambient in minutes (TAA); and 4) percentage

time above ambient (%TAA). These descriptors were analyzed on a logarithmic scale, which was found to perform best in dose-response regressions. For exploratory purposes, each time-based descriptor was segmented into portions based on which type of aircraft was present from a predetermined aircraft hierarchy order (Helicopter tour, general aviation tour, high altitude jet overflight, or unknown). In other words, if both a helicopter tour and a high altitude jet were present at the same time, the event was logged as a helicopter tour.

Level-Based Descriptors: 1) aircraft equivalent sound level ($L_{Aeq,Tac}$); 2) aircraft equivalent sound level normalized to the respondents' duration ($L_{Aeq,Tresp}$); 3) aircraft equivalent sound level normalized to a one-hour time period ($L_{Aeq,1h}$); 4) change in sound exposure due to aircraft ($\Delta L_{AE,Tac}$); 5) change in sound exposure due to aircraft normalized to the respondent's duration ($\Delta L_{AE,Tresp}$); and 6) maximum aircraft sound level (L_{ASmx}).

Event-Based Descriptors: 1) the number of aircraft (NUM_{ac}); and 2) the number of aircraft per hour ($NUM_{ac/hr}$).

1.2.2 Visitor Response

Park visitor reaction to aircraft noise was quantified based on the responses to two questions within the study questionnaire. The questions, "Were you bothered or annoyed by aircraft noise during your visit to the site?" and "How much did the sound from aircraft interfere with your enjoyment of the site?", were answered by rating annoyance / interference with enjoyment on a five point scale, labeled 1) not at all, 2) slightly, 3) moderately, 4) very much, or 5) extremely annoyed / interfered. Appendix B presents a statistical summary of the responses to these and other pertinent questions.

The nature of the logistic response regression (see Section 2.1) requires that the answer to these two key questions be dichotomized, or split into two groups: either 'yes', the response is present, or 'no' the response is not present. The determination of which points on the response scale are to be categorized as yes/no requires knowledge of what type of response is to be measured and is usually left open to the researcher responsible for the analysis.

In previous studies for the NPS, visitor response was dichotomized by categorizing the top three responses (moderately, very much and extremely) as "annoyed", and the bottom two (slightly and not at all) as "not annoyed". However, the FAA and others have historically categorized the top two responses (very much and extremely) as "highly annoyed", and the bottom three (moderately, slightly, and not at all) as "not highly annoyed".

The use of the highly annoyed dichotomization dates back to the community response work of Schultz[4]. Because Schultz's work was a synthesis of many different surveys, in which the number of steps in the response scale and the labeling of the steps differed, the choice of response dichotomization was somewhat complex. It would appear that Schultz chose the concept of highly annoyed because it was reasonably clear as to which points should be included on the differing scales of the various studies he examined. In contrast, the concept of moderate annoyance in Schulz's case would not have allowed for such clear-cut decisions to be made, since the clarity of which points to categorize as moderately-annoyed across the various studies was somewhat ambiguous. Since the studies examined herein provided for a clear distinction between slight, moderate and high annoyance, top 4, top 3 and top 2, respectively, investigations are conducted in Section 2.2 to determine if the selection can be clearly justified through appropriate statistical tests.

1.3 Report Organization

Section 1 contains an introduction and overview of the data used in this report. Sections 2.1 and 2.2 contain an overview of the dose-response methodology, and a summary of several exploratory analyses. Section 2.3 contains a summary of the analysis methods used to compare dose-response data between different sites and different parks. Section 3 presents a summary of the results of the analyses presented in Section 2.3. Section 4 explores the dose-response relationships for the eight acoustic descriptors and presents an example of how these descriptors could be combined for practical use.

2.0 METHODOLOGY

2.1 Framework
Park visitors' reactions were identified by relating noise (dose) and visitor response (annoyance or interference) mathematically through regression. The chosen method of regression was Logistic Dose-Response Regression, the form of which is:

$$\% Annoyance\,/\,Interference = 100\left(\frac{e^{b_0 + b_1\left(AcousticDescriptor\right)}}{1 + e^{b_0 + b_1\left(AcousticDescriptor\right)}} \right)$$

where: b_0 is the constant of the regression; and
b_1 is the coefficient of the acoustic descriptor.

This type of regression ensures that the predicted response probability will fall between 0 and 100 percent, and is a common analysis technique in dose-response studies.

2.2 Exploratory Analysis for Overlooks and Short Hikes
During the exploratory phase of the analysis, data from the seven overlook sites were combined as one set, as were data from the four retained short hike sites. In Section 2.3, analysis is conducted to determine if these combinations are statistically valid.

2.2.1 Comparison of Annoyance and Interference with Enjoyment
This analysis focused on the first key question, "Is visitor response to the 'annoyance' question different from visitor response to the 'interference' question (i.e., "Were you bothered or annoyed by aircraft noise during your visit to the site?" versus "How much did the sound from aircraft interfere with your enjoyment of the site?")?". Previous discussions have suggested that rather than predict visitor response based on answers to the 'annoyance' question, visitor response should be based on answers to the 'interference' question. A t-test for dependent samples was performed using the values denoting the answers to these questions to determine if responses varied significantly between the two. This type of test is performed if the two groups of measurements that are to be compared are based on the same set of respondents[5]. The average of the difference between these variables for short hike respondents was 0.16, while the average for overlook respondents was 0.04. These averages indicate that both sets of respondents rate annoyance slightly higher than interference with enjoyment. The results of the T-tests show that the difference for both groups is significant at the 0.05 level.

Although annoyance and interference with enjoyment were determined to be statistically different, practically, they are very close in terms of visitor response. Table 4 presents this data in a slightly different manner, showing that the vast majority of respondents rate annoyance equal to or higher than interference with enjoyment (consistent with the statistical findings above), signifying that use of annoyance, if anything, provides for a more conservative assessment (i.e., with annoyance, visitors would expect to be impacted at lower levels as compared with interference with enjoyment). Based on these results, enjoyment and annoyance are considered interchangeable (and hence treated equally) for subsequent analysis. The presented results are based on responses to the annoyance question.

Table 4. Comparison of Answers to Enjoyment vs. Annoyance Questions

Percentage of Visitors who:	Short Hikes	Overlooks
Rate Enjoyment and Annoyance Equal	71.5%	86.0%
Rate Annoyance Higher	20.9%	8.4%
Rate Enjoyment Higher	7.6%	5.6%

2.2.2 Dichotomization of the Annoyance Scale

This analysis focused on the second key question: *Should visitor response be dichotomized based on the top two of five steps on the response scale, the top three, or the top four?* A statistical analysis was performed to determine if there is clear justification for the choice of response dichotomization. This analysis utilized a goodness-of-fit statistic and a reliability statistic[§]. The analysis, presented in Appendix C, was conducted for each of the twelve acoustic descriptors, using the following visitor response dichotomizations:

    1) The top two responses to the annoyance question
    2) The top three responses to the annoyance question
    3) The top four responses to the annoyance question

The goodness-of-fit statistics reported in the Appendix are extremely close, and in many cases, equal for the three dichotomizations. For overlooks, the top two dichotomization may provide a better fit for %TA and %TAA, while the top three dichotomization may provide a better fit for $L_{Aeq,1h}$. No one dichotomization provides a better fit for the remaining descriptors for overlooks or any of the descriptors for short hikes. As a result, it is not appropriate to report that one dichotomization provides for a better regression fit.

The reliability analysis shows that the top four dichotomization is most reliable for the level-based descriptors, while the top three is most reliable for the majority of the time-based and number based descriptors. Also worthy of note is that, when using the top two dichotomization for overlooks, the coefficient of the acoustic descriptor almost never achieves a 5% significance level. This is due to the low occurrence of highly annoyed respondents, which results in an essentially 'flat' dose-response curve.

When goodness-of-fit and reliability are considered together, no one dichotomization can be said to perform well in both tests. The dose-response curves in the following Figure and Appendix D are presented for response dichotomizations that use both the top two (as used in residential studies) and the top three (as used in previous park visitor response studies).

[§] Additional analysis techniques, such as cluster analysis, may be used in future investigations to determine if a clear justification is present.

When regression curves using the top three dichotomization are compared to those using the top two dichotomization, the relationships show significantly higher levels of annoyance for the same amount of aircraft noise. For example, Figure 1 predicts that, for short hikes, 20% of visitors would respond as moderately to extremely annoyed (top 3) at levels above 9% TAA, while the same percentage (20%) of visitors would respond as very to extremely annoyed (top 2) at levels of 100% TAA.

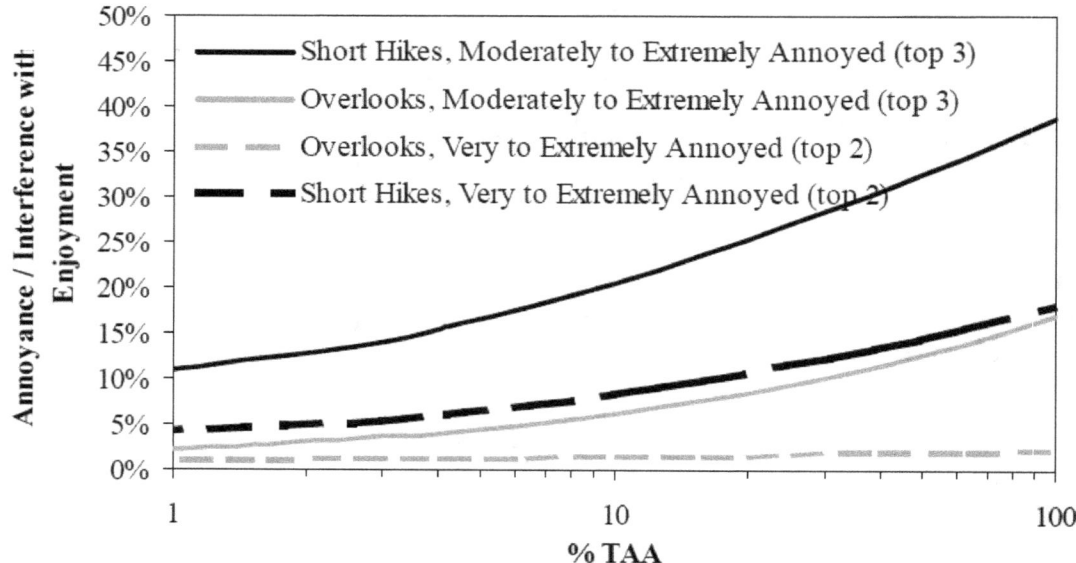

Figure 1. Comparison of Response Dichotomizations

2.2.3 Comparison of Response to Noise, with and without High-Altitude Jets

This analysis focused on the fourth key question, "Is there any evidence that visitors are annoyed by high altitude jet overflight noise?". During the calculation of the time-based acoustic dose descriptors, each descriptor was segmented into portions based on which type of aircraft (Helicopter tour, general aviation tour, high altitude jet overflight, or unknown aircraft) was the predominant contributor. The visitor responses corresponding to visits during which there was only high altitude aircraft audible for the entire duration were examined. Table 5 presents an overview of the responses of these visitors as compared to the visitors who were exposed to tour aircraft and high altitude jet noise combined.

Table 5 Overview of Responses, Tour Aircraft + Jet and Jet Only

	Overlook		Short Hike	
	Tour Aircraft + Jet	Jet Only	Tour Aircraft + Jet	Jet Only
Number of Respondents	785	150	1122	50
Percentage who reported hearing aircraft when noise dose >0	45%	17%	77%	55%
Percentage who reported moderate to extreme annoyance when noise dose >0	11%	4%	30%	10%
Percentage who reported very or extreme annoyance when noise dose >0	3%	1%	14%	6%

This table shows that visitors may be more sensitive to tour aircraft as compared with high-altitude jets. To further explore this possibility, Figures 2 and 3 show the average annoyance responses and corresponding 95% confidence intervals as a function of both %TAA and $L_{Aeq,1h}$ in 10 %/dbA bins.

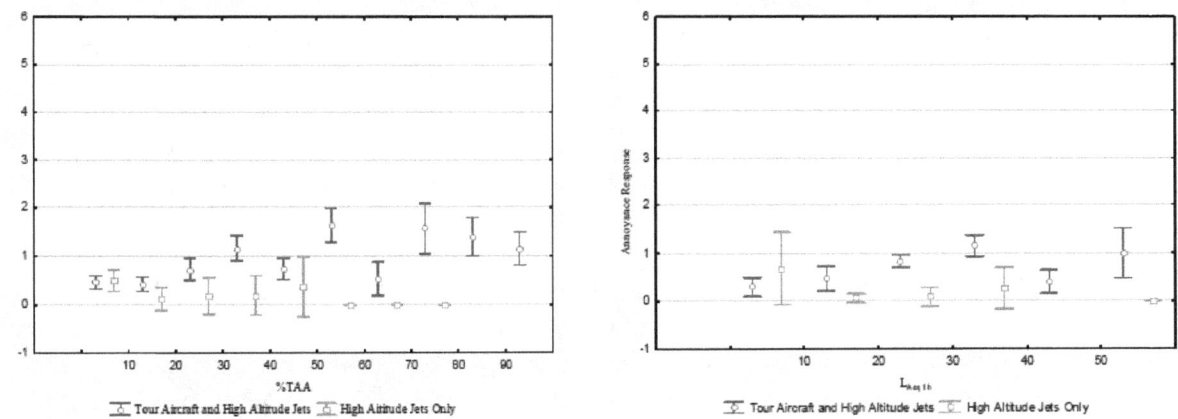

Figure 2 Average Annoyance Responses, Overlooks

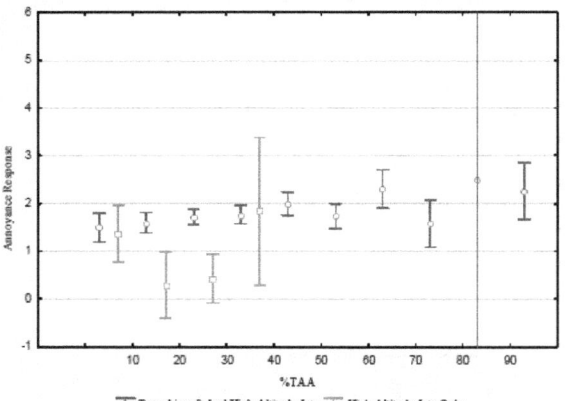 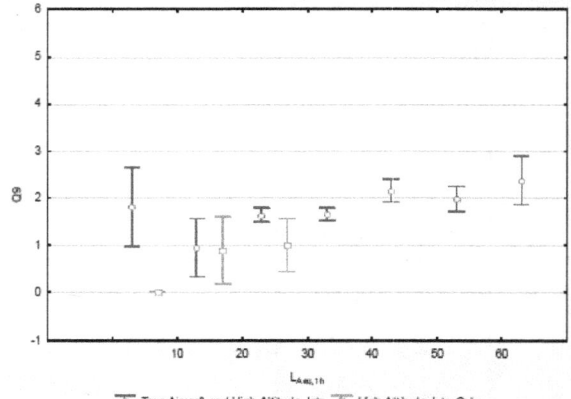

Figure 3. Average Annoyance Responses, Short Hikes

These graphics show that, although the average responses for the jet-only respondents are lower, not all of the data 'bins' show this with statistical certainty. Therefore, no definitive conclusions can be drawn. Consequently, all subsequent analyses treat aircraft noise in the aggregate (high altitude jets and air tours combined), recognizing that air tour noise is the dominant contributor for the data included herein.

2.2.4 Determination of Significant Acoustic Descriptors

In order to streamline the analysis process, it was decided that only the acoustic descriptors with the best relative performance would be carried forward. To measure performance, a logistic regression analysis was performed for short hikes and overlooks for each of the 12 acoustic descriptors. A summary of this analysis can be found in Appendix E. The performance of each descriptor was evaluated for both overlooks and short hikes based on its goodness of fit statistic, %Concordance, and Reliability[1].

This analysis showed that, generally, the time-based descriptors performed the best, followed by the level-based descriptors, with the event-based descriptors performing least best of the three types of descriptors. Eight out of the twelve acoustic descriptors rated first, second or third in at least one performance category: %TA, TAA, %TAA, $L_{Aeq,1h}$, $L_{Aeq,Tresp}$, $\Delta L_{AE,Tac}$, $\Delta L_{AE,Tresp}$, and NUMac. These descriptors (which included one from each of the three basic descriptor types: event, time, and level) were retained for further analysis.

2.2.5 Sensitivity Analysis of the Effect of Ambient Sound Levels

The analysis described in the previous section showed that the change in exposure descriptors, $\Delta L_{AE,Tac}$ and $\Delta L_{AE,Tresp}$, may be among the good predictors of visitor response in a park environment. This Section will explore 1) the validity of this finding (Section 2.2.5.1), and 2) the effect of differing methods of computing ambient sound level on the dose-response relationships (Section 2.2.5.2).

2.2.5.1 Using Ambient as a Covariate

The conclusion that $\Delta L_{AE,Tac}$ and $\Delta L_{AE,Tresp}$ may be good predictors of visitor reaction in a park environment seems to be in conflict with dose-response studies conducted in a residential environment. These studies have shown that *residents'* reactions to audible environmental noise cannot be reliably predicted using change in exposure descriptors.[6] However, the real question is, "Do residents' reactions correlate well with park visitor reactions?".

In order to test the strength of the change in exposure descriptors in a park environment, ambient noise (which is inherent in the calculation of the change in exposure descriptors) was isolated and instead added as a covariate to the regressions for $L_{Aeq,Tresp}$ and $L_{Aeq,1h}$. If the ambient noise level covariate is negative and significant at the .05 Chi^2 level, it can be said that increasing levels of ambient noise would decrease park visitors' annoyance to aircraft overflights, i.e., the reactions of park visitors, unlike those of residential communities, could be reliably predicted using a change in exposure descriptor.

Three different descriptors for quantifying ambient noise levels were considered:1) The equivalent non-aircraft noise level during the respondents' visit ($L_{Aeq,Tamb}$), 2) The non-aircraft noise level (i.e., traditional ambient) that was exceeded 50 percent of the time during the hour of the respondents' visit (L_{50}), and 3) The non-aircraft noise level (i.e., traditional ambient) that was exceeded 90 percent of the time during the hour of the respondents' visit (L_{90}).

Table 6 and Table 7 present the pertinent results of the logistic regression analyses performed for each acoustic descriptor for overlooks and short hikes, respectively. Presented are the coefficient of the acoustic descriptor, whether or not that coefficient is significant (if it was significant, and at what significance level), the coefficient of the covariate, $L_{Aeq,Tamb}$, L_{50}, or L_{90}, whether or not that coefficient is significant (if it was significant, and at what significance level), and the Pearson Chi^2 statistic divided by the number of degrees of freedom (dof). The significance level represents the level of confidence that the determination of significance is correct, (e.g., if b_1 is determined to be significant at a level of .05, then one can be 95 percent certain the coefficient is significant). The Pearson Chi^2 is a criteria used to judge the "goodness of fit" of the model, taking into account the effect of different sample sizes and different numbers of variables. In general, the lower the statistic, the better the model fit. Therefore, it provides a measure of relative "goodness" of models developed for individual noise descriptors.

Table 6. Leq + Ambient Logistic Regression Results, Overlooks

Acoustic Descriptor	Coefficient	Coefficient Significant?	Ambient Descriptor	Coefficient	Coefficient Significant?	Pearson Chi²/dof
$L_{Aeq,Tresp}$	0.032	Yes**				0.996
$L_{Aeq,Tresp}$	0.058	Yes**	$L_{Aeq,Tamb}$	-0.069	Yes*	0.974
$L_{Aeq,Tresp}$	0.050	Yes***	L_{50}	-0.092	Yes***	0.991
$L_{Aeq,Tresp}$	0.040	Yes**	L_{90}	-0.064	Yes*	1.002
$L_{Aeq,1h}$	0.037	Yes**				0.971
$L_{Aeq,1h}$	0.072	Yes***	$L_{Aeq,Tamb}$	-0.083	Yes**	0.944
$L_{Aeq,1h}$	0.052	Yes***	L_{50}	-0.085	Yes**	0.967
$L_{Aeq,1h}$	0.043	Yes***	L_{90}	-0.058	Yes*	0.974

*Significant at .05 (95% Certainty)   **Significant at .01 (99% Certainty)   ***Significant at .001 (99.9% Certainty)

Table 7. Leq + Ambient Logistic Regression Results, Short Hikes

Acoustic Descriptor	Coefficient	Coefficient Significant?	Ambient Descriptor	Coefficient	Coefficient Significant?	Pearson Chi²/dof
$L_{Aeq,Tresp}$	0.009	No				1.001
$L_{Aeq,Tresp}$	0.032	Yes**	$L_{Aeq,Tamb}$	-0.038	Yes**	1.001
$L_{Aeq,Tresp}$	0.018	Yes*	L_{50}	-0.035	Yes**	1.003
$L_{Aeq,Tresp}$	0.016	Yes*	L_{90}	-0.030	Yes**	1.002
$L_{Aeq,1h}$	0.006	No				1.002
$L_{Aeq,1h}$	0.025	Yes**	$L_{Aeq,Tamb}$	-0.035	Yes*	1.002
$L_{Aeq,1h}$	0.013	No	L_{50}	-0.032	Yes**	1.003
$L_{Aeq,1h}$	0.011	No	L_{90}	-0.028	Yes*	1.003

*Significant at .05 (95% Certainty)   **Significant at .01 (99% Certainty)   ***Significant at .001 (99.9% Certainty)

In all cases, the ambient covariates are significant, indicating that their inclusion increases the accuracy of the predicted visitor annoyance. For overlooks, they also increase the significance of the acoustic descriptor and the goodness of fit. For short hikes, however, all three increase the significance of $L_{Aeq,Tresp}$, but only $L_{Aeq,Tamb}$ increases the significance of $L_{Aeq,1h}$, and in no instances do they increase the goodness of fit. Overall, $L_{Aeq,Tamb}$ seems the best choice for quantifying the ambient sound level. While $L_{Aeq,Tamb}$ may be the best descriptor that defines ambient sound level, it may not be practical to calculate this descriptor under some circumstances, since much of the available park noise data will not be collected with observers continually present. Rather L_{50} and L_{90} may be more practical, since they do not require the presence of an observer. Tables 6 and 7 also show that in the absence of $L_{Aeq,Tamb}$, L_{50} may be the next-best choice, based on its ability to improve the significance of the acoustic descriptor.

While it has been reported that ambient noise is not a good predictor of residential annoyance, it seems that it is indeed a good predictor of park visitor annoyance. The reasons for this difference are not entirely understood, but may lie in the fundamental differences in attitudes between long-term residential annoyance and short-term park visitor annoyance. In addition, ambient sound levels in the parks are typically much lower than those in residential environments. Ambient sound levels range between 10 and 60 dB at overlooks and between 10 and 50 dB at short hikes, while the majority of ambient sound levels in residential environments range from between 45 and 70 dB in residential environments[6].

2.2.5.2 The Effect of Different Definitions of Ambient

The previous Sections report that the inclusion of all three forms of ambient, whether inherent in the acoustic descriptor or added as a covariate, increase the accuracy of the predicted visitor annoyance. Therefore, it is desirable to examine if the use of these definitions of ambient sound level in the calculation of the change in exposure descriptors results in significantly different dose-response relationships.

The change in exposure descriptors, $\Delta L_{AE,Tac}$, and $\Delta L_{AE,Tresp}$, were calculated using both L_{50} ($\Delta L_{AE,Tac,L50}$ and $\Delta L_{AE,Tresp,L50}$) and L_{90} ($\Delta L_{AE,Tac,L90}$ and $\Delta L_{AE,Tresp,L90}$) rather than $L_{Aeq,Tamb}$, and the logistic dose-response relationships were computed for each. Figure 4, Figure 5, Figure 6, and Figure 7 graphically show that the differences between the relationships are not statistically significant, indicated by the overlapping 95% Confidence Intervals.

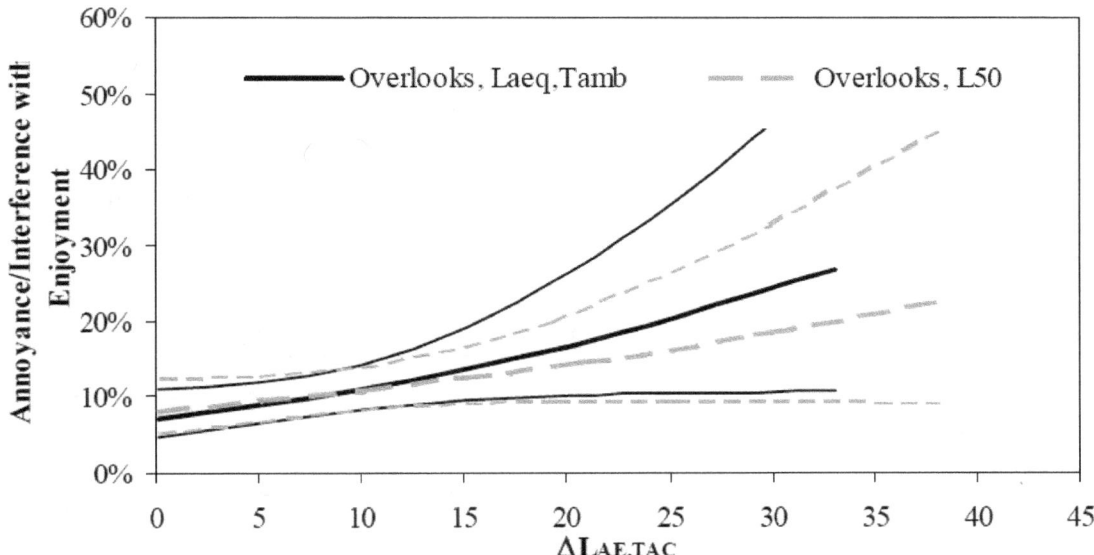

Figure 4. Dose-Response Relationships for Overlooks
Using $\Delta L_{AE,Tac}$ and $\Delta L_{AE,Tac,L50}$

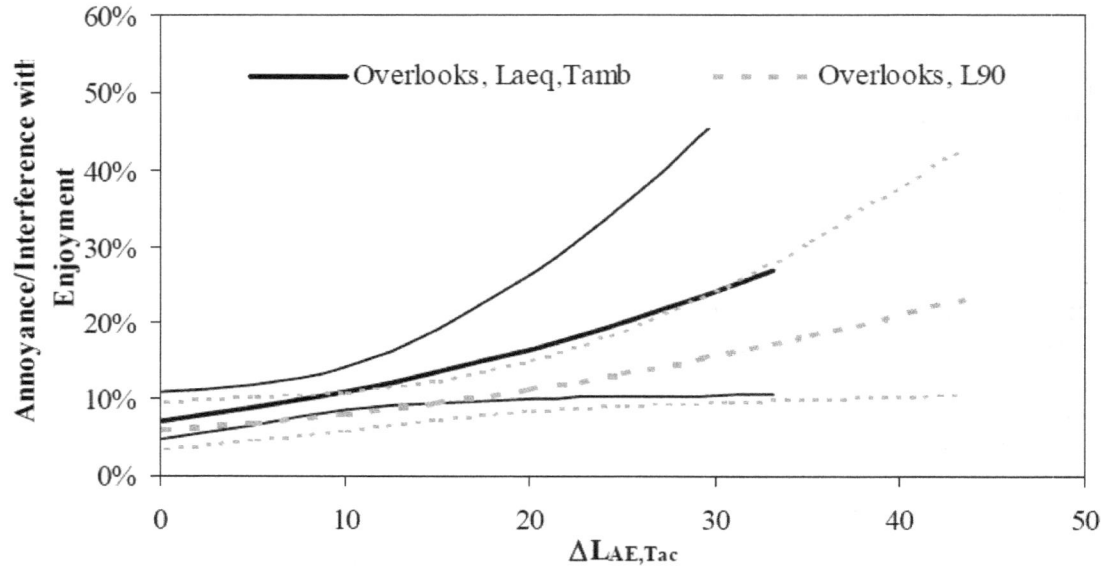

**Figure 5. Dose-Response Relationships for Overlooks
Using $\Delta L_{AE,Tac}$ and $\Delta L_{AE,Tac,90}$**

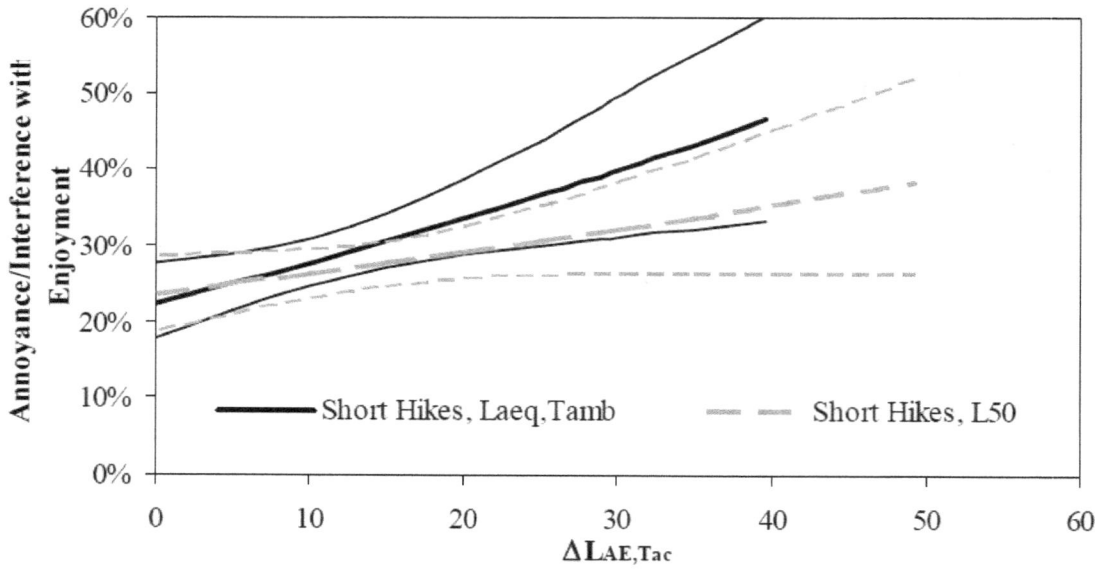

**Figure 6. Dose-Response Relationships for Short Hikes
Using $\Delta L_{AE,Tac}$ and $\Delta L_{AE,Tac,50}$**

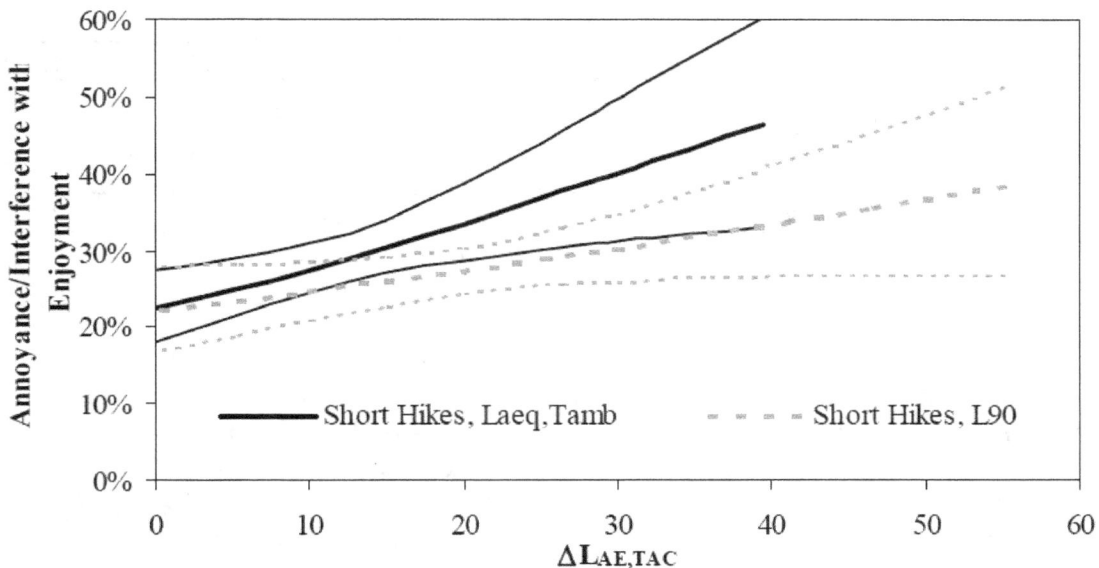

Figure 7. Dose-Response Relationships for Short Hikes
Using $\Delta L_{AE,Tac}$ and $\Delta L_{AE,Tac,90}$

2.3 Site-Based Comparisons

Questions 4, 5, and 6 in Section 1.0 all require comparisons based on specific site characteristics or location. Comparisons were made statistically by introducing a covariate based on site into the logistic regression. By introducing this variable, we ask the question: "Can the variation in visitor response be explained, not only by acoustic dose, but also by site-specific characteristics?" If the addition of the site covariate did not significantly improve the fit of the model, it can be said that there is no basis to include this term in the model[7] (i.e., none of the variation in response can be explained by this variable). This statistical analysis technique is commonplace in the literature, and was used in previous park dose-response studies[3].

If there was no basis to include the site covariate in the model, it can be said that there is statistically no difference between sites (i.e., the sites are statistically similar). The test for inclusion of the site covariate was performed for each of the eight retained acoustic descriptors (%TA, TAA, %TAA, $L_{Aeq,Tresp}$, $L_{Aeq,1h}$, $\Delta L_{AE,Tac}$, $\Delta L_{AE,Tresp}$, and NUMac). Sites were merged if at least six of the eight tests showed there was no difference between sites.

2.3.1 Site-Site Comparisons

The site-site analysis focused on the third key question: "Is visitor response to tour aircraft overflight noise similar for sites of the same type (i.e., overlook versus short hike sites) within the same park?". Table 8 shows the possible site combinations and the results of similarity tests, as discussed above.

Table 8. Same-Park Site Groupings

Site Type	Park	Sites	Similar?
Overlook	Bryce Canyon	Rainbow Point and Fairyland	Yes
Overlook	Bryce Canyon	Rainbow Point and Bryce Point	Yes
Overlook	Grand Canyon (SR)	Lipan Point and Pima Point	Yes
Overlook	Grand Canyon (NR)	Point Imperial 92 and Point Imperial 99	Yes
Short Hike	Bryce Canyon	Queens Garden and Queens Garden Extended	Yes

This table shows that, in all cases, sites of the same type within a park are statistically similar. In addition, this analysis provides a positive answer to the seventh key question (Section 1.0), "Does visitor response to tour aircraft overflight noise at the same location change over time?". By treating the data from each year as a separate 'site', the analysis showed that there was no basis for the inclusion of a 'site' covariate. Consequentially, it can be concluded that there was no change in visitor response between the years 1992 and 1999, at least for data taken at Point Imperial on the North Rim of the Grand Canyon.

2.3.2 Park-Park Comparisons

This analysis focused on the fourth key question: "Is visitor response to tour aircraft overflight noise similar for different parks?". A preliminary analysis showed that: 1) overlook sites at Bryce Canyon and Grand Canyon (NR) are similar, while both are dissimilar to Grand Canyon (SR); and 2) short hike sites *may be* dissimilar at all three parks. Further analysis of other variables (covariates) was undertaken in Subsections 2.3.2.1 through 2.3.2.3 to determine if there were fundamental differences among visitors from park to park that would help explain the apparent dissimilarities at short hike sites.

2.3.2.1 Visit Duration Analysis

It was found that, although sites at Bryce Canyon, Haleakala, and Hawaii Volcanoes were all classified as short hikes and had similar *average* visit durations; the distributions of visit duration were actually quite dissimilar. Figure 8, Figure 9, and Figure 10 show the distributions of visit duration at Bryce Canyon, Haleakala, and Hawaii Volcanoes, respectively.

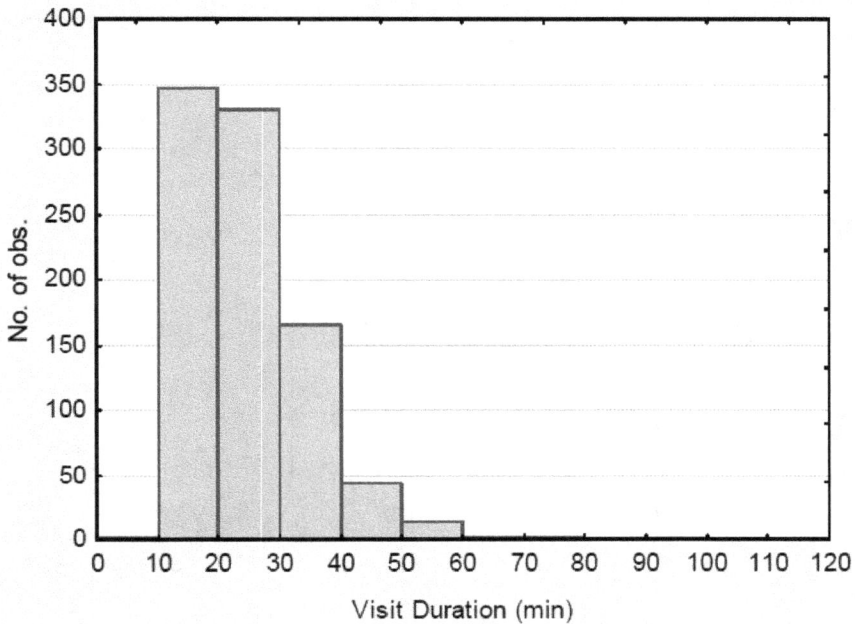

Figure 8. Distribution of Visit Duration at Bryce Canyon

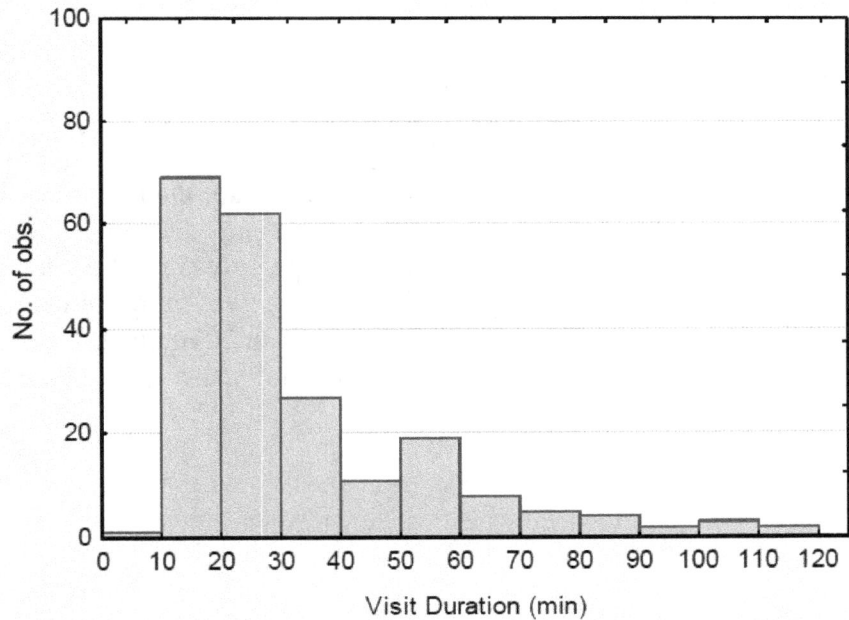

Figure 9. Distribution of Visit Duration at Haleakala

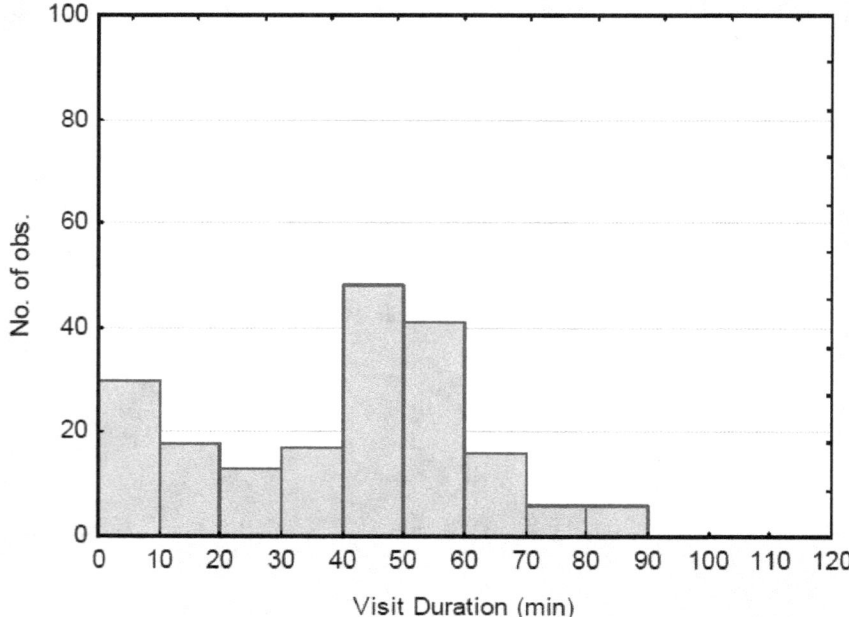

Figure 10. Distribution of Visit Duration at Hawaii Volcanoes

Figures 8 and 9 show that visits to both Bryce Canyon and Haleakala have a leftward skew with regard to time. The Hawaii Volcanoes data in Figure 10 appear to show that there may have been two distinct groups of visitors represented in the Hawaii Volcanoes data. Further investigation of the data revealed the visitor behavior that resulted in these groupings. As noted by an observer stationed at the end of the trail, most visitors (131 out of 195) completed the hike from the beginning to end of the trail. The remainder seemingly spent a limited amount of time sightseeing only around the trailhead; they were not observed at the end of the trail. Figure 11 shows that those who were not observed at the end of the trail generally spent less than 20 minutes at the site, while those who were observed at the end of the trail generally spent more than 20 minutes at the site.

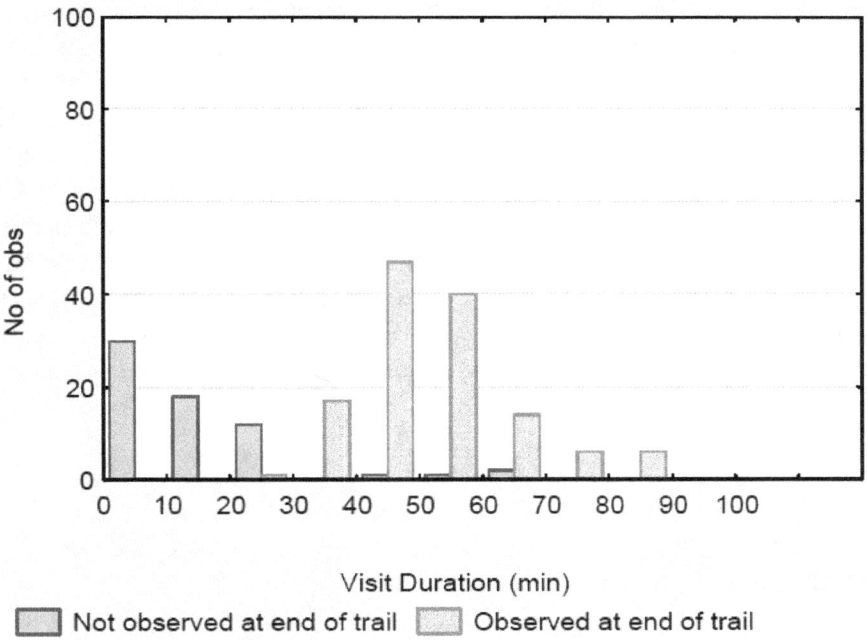

Figure 11 Distribution of Visit Duration by Trail Completion at Hawaii Volcanoes

In order to provide for a valid comparison between parks, it was decided that visitors who did not complete the entire hike should not be classified as short hike respondents and were excluded from further analysis. To remain consistent, only visitors at Haleakala who were interviewed at the end of the trail, or completed the entire top-to-bottom round trip hike (179 out of 213) were included in the analysis. All visitors at Bryce Canyon were included; they were interviewed only at the end of trail.

Exclusion of these respondents resulted in a significant improvement in the performance of each logistic regression, while also increasing the evidence of park-park similarities (i.e., a larger portion of the eight acoustic descriptors showed that the parks were similar, but not enough (<6) to classify the parks as statistically similar). Consequentially, further investigation was done to explore the dissimilarities.

2.3.2.2 Covariate Analysis
To explore the remaining variance in visitor response at short hike sites between parks, an analysis of ten covariates was performed. The covariates included: number of adults in group, number of children in group, total number of people in group, first visit to site (yes/no), importance of scenery for visit (rated 1 to 5), importance of natural quiet for visit (rated 1 to 5), importance of history for visit (rated 1 to 5), gender, year born, and US citizenship (yes/no). Statistical comparisons were conducted by introducing each covariate individually into the regression. By introducing these variables, we ask the question: Can some of the variation in visitor response be explained not only by acoustic dose, but also by the covariates?

This analysis of covariates showed that significant differences exist between first time visitors and repeat visitors. Repeat visitors generally report more annoyance/interference than first-time visitors. In general, an additional ten percent of repeat visitors will be annoyed by the same dose of aircraft noise at short hike sites, while an additional two to ten percent of repeat visitors will be annoyed by the same dose of aircraft noise at overlooks. This variation in increased annoyance at overlooks is a function of dose, with the largest increases being associated with the largest dose. Additionally, reasons for visit such as to enjoy the natural quiet or historical significance can affect response, although to a lesser degree. Factors such as number of people and number of children in the group may have slight influences but are not significant enough to warrant further study. Due to the increased complexity of adding covariates to the relationships, only the first visit covariate was considered for further analysis.

2.3.2.3 Conclusion

Short hike sites at all three parks were found to be statistically similar and could be definitively combined by limiting the respondents to only those who had completed the entire hike and by including first visit as a covariate (see Table 9).

Table 9. Park-Park Site Groupings

Site Type	Park	Similar?
Short Hike	Bryce Canyon (QGT, QGTX) and Haleakala (SS)	Yes
Short Hike	Bryce Canyon (QGT, QGTX) and Hawaii Volcanoes (WT)	Yes
Short Hike	Haleakala (SS) and Hawaii Volcanoes (WT)	Yes

2.4 Final Format of Dose-Response Regression

The final dose response regression includes first visit as a covariate for both short hikes and overlooks. The resulting form of the equation is:

$$\% Annoyance / Interference = 100 \left(\frac{e^{b_0 + b_1 (AcousticDescriptor) + b_2 (FirstVisitVariable)}}{1 + e^{b_0 + b_1 (AcousticDescriptor) + b_2 (FirstVisitoVariable)}} \right)$$

where: b_0 is the constant of the regression,
b_1 is the coefficient of the acoustic descriptor; and
b_2 is the coefficient of the first visit variable (1 for first time visitors and 2 for repeat visitors).

2.5 Final Determination of Significant Acoustic Descriptors

As a result of the analyses of Section 2.3, the size of the final dataset and the format of the logistic regression were altered. The performance of the eight acoustic descriptors was re-evaluated to determine if their relative performance had changed. A logistic regression analysis identical to that described in Appendix E was performed for short hikes and overlooks (combined) for each retained acoustic descriptor. The results of this analysis are summarized in Appendix F.

This analysis showed that the relative performance of the eight descriptors did change slightly. Three level based descriptors, $L_{Aeq,1h}$, $\Delta L_{AE,Tac}$, and $\Delta L_{AE,Tresp}$, improved in performance while the performance of the time-based descriptors, %TA, TAA and %TAA was degraded. The descriptors that showed the best overall performance (in terms of the criteria presented in Table F-5) were %TAA, $L_{Aeq,1h}$, $\Delta L_{AE,Tac}$, and $\Delta L_{AE,Tresp}$. When the site types are considered separately, the descriptors that showed the best performance for overlooks were %TAA and $L_{Aeq,1h}$. For short hikes, the best descriptors were $\Delta L_{AE,Tac}$ and $\Delta L_{AE,Tresp}$. Graphical presentations of the final dose-response curves are displayed in Appendix D for all eight acoustic descriptors.

2.6 Limitations

Due to the underlying nature of the data used in this analysis, there are a number of items that should be considered before applying the dose-response relationships presented herein to other park environments.

- Ambient sound levels in the parks in this study ranged between 10 and 40 dBA. The appropriateness of applying these relationships to parks with ambient levels above about 40 dBA is not clear.
- The methodology presented herein only applies to assessment of noise impact on park visitors. Special considerations will have to be given to wildlife and cultural impacts.
- The majority of the data underlying the short hike curves was measured at BCNP. This data consists, almost exclusively, of helicopter tours using a Bell 206L.
- There are underlying site biases that may influence the dose-response curves. Appendix G discusses these biases and the certainty of the dose-response curves at the upper and lower bounds.

3.0 ANALYSIS SUMMARY

The following section summarizes the answers to the key questions presented in the introduction. Graphics in this Section are presented using 1) the %TAA descriptor (best performing) and 2) the top three dichotomization of visitor response (from previous NPS studies).

Is visitor response to the 'annoyance' question different from visitor response to the 'interference' question (i.e., "Were you bothered or annoyed by aircraft noise during your visit to the site?" versus "How much did the sound from aircraft interfere with your enjoyment of the site?")?

The vast majority of visitors (92.4% to 94.4%) rate annoyance equal to or higher than interference with enjoyment, signifying that use of annoyance, if anything, provides for a more conservative assessment (i.e., with annoyance, visitors would expect to be impacted at lower levels as compared with interference with enjoyment). Based on these results, annoyance responses were used for all analyses presented herein. The dose-response relationships for interference with enjoyment are assumed to be equivalent.

Should visitor response be dichotomized based on the top two of five steps on the response scale, the top three, or the top four?

No one dichotomization can be said to perform well in both statistical goodness-of-fit and reliability tests. Therefore, there is no definitive scientific evidence present to reliably choose a dichotomization. As a result, the dose-response curves are presented for response dichotomizations that use both the top three (as used in previous park visitor response studies) and the top two (as used in residential studies) dichotomizations.

Is there any evidence that visitors are less annoyed by high altitude jet overflight noise than by tour aircraft overflight noise?

Visitors appear to be less sensitive to high-altitude jet overflight noise as compared with noise from tour aircraft. However, the data does not show this with statistical certainty and no definitive conclusions can be drawn. Consequently, all analyses presented herein treat aircraft noise in the aggregate (high altitude jets and air tours combined), recognizing that air tour noise is the dominant contributor to the overall aircraft sound level for the data included herein.

Is visitor response to tour aircraft overflight noise similar for sites of the same type (i.e., overlook versus short hike sites) within the same park?

The following were proven to be similar:
Bryce Canyon overlooks: Bryce Point, Rainbow Point and Fairyland.
Grand Canyon (SR) overlooks: Pima Point and Lipan Point
Grand Canyon (NR) overlooks: Point Imperial 1999 and Point Imperial 1992
Bryce Canyon short hikes: Queens Garden and Queens Garden Extended

Is visitor response to tour aircraft overflight noise similar for different parks?

Overlooks: It was found that while overlook sites at Bryce Canyon and Grand Canyon (NR) are statistically similar, there were differences between these sites and Grand Canyon (SR). Figure 12 shows the annoyance difference ranges from 2% at 10% TAA to 15% at 100% TAA. Figure 12 also shows that the 95% Confidence Intervals overlap between 1 and 35% TAA, and are very close to overlap for values of TAA above 35%. Therefore, although the difference between these two groups of sites is statistically significant, it may not be a practical enough difference upon which to base separate dose-response curves, given the required added complexity. Subsequent Sections of this document combine data from the two sets of overlook sites.

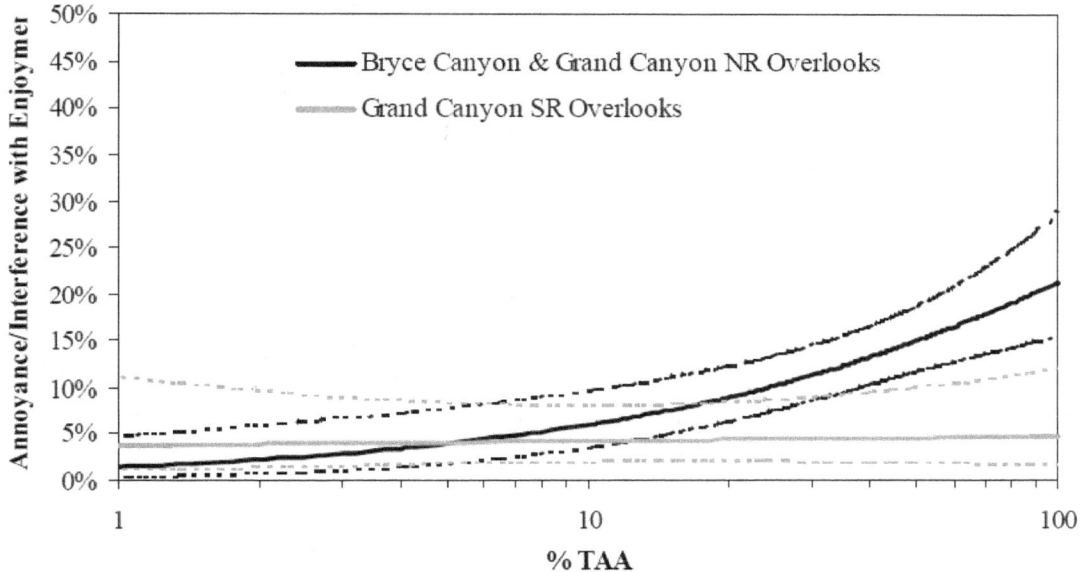

Figure 12. Overlook Dose-Response Curves
Grand Canyon SR vs. Grand Canyon NR and Bryce Canyon

Short Hikes: Preliminary analysis showed dissimilarities among all three parks. Further analysis showed that the short hike sites were found to be statistically similar at different parks and could be combined by limiting the respondents to those who completed the entire hike and by including first visit as a covariate. Figure 13 shows that the curves cross and the 95% confidence intervals overlap throughout the range of available data.

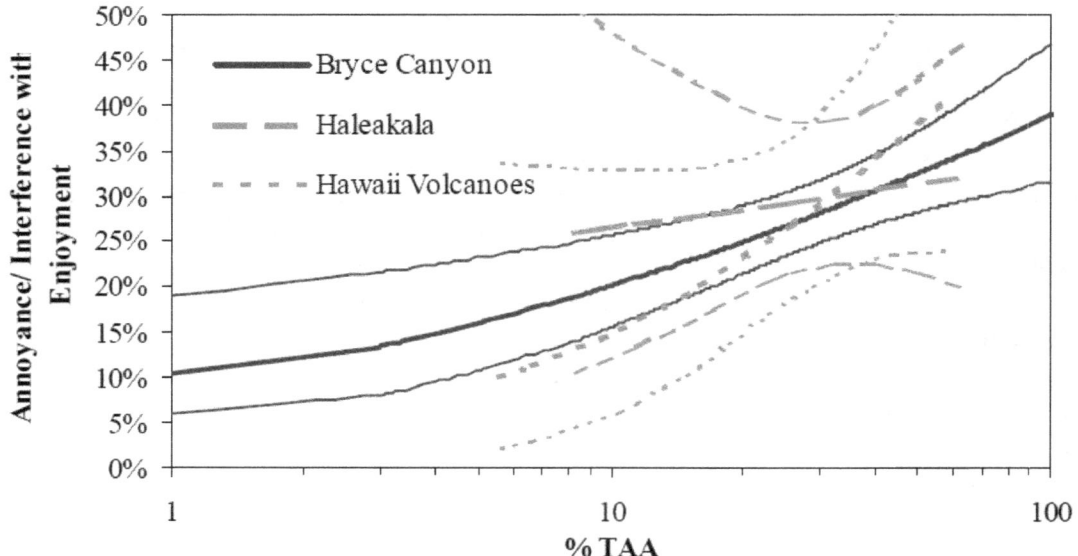

Figure 13. Short Hike Dose-Response Curves
Bryce Canyon, Haleakala, and Hawaii Volcanoes

Is visitor response to tour aircraft overflight noise similar at different types of sites (i.e., overlook versus short hike) for different parks?

No, Figure 14 shows graphically the difference between the two types of sites. In this figure, the overlook curve includes the combined data from Bryce Canyon, Grand Canyon (NR), *and* Grand Canyon (SR). It can be seen that at no point do the 95% Confidence Intervals overlap.

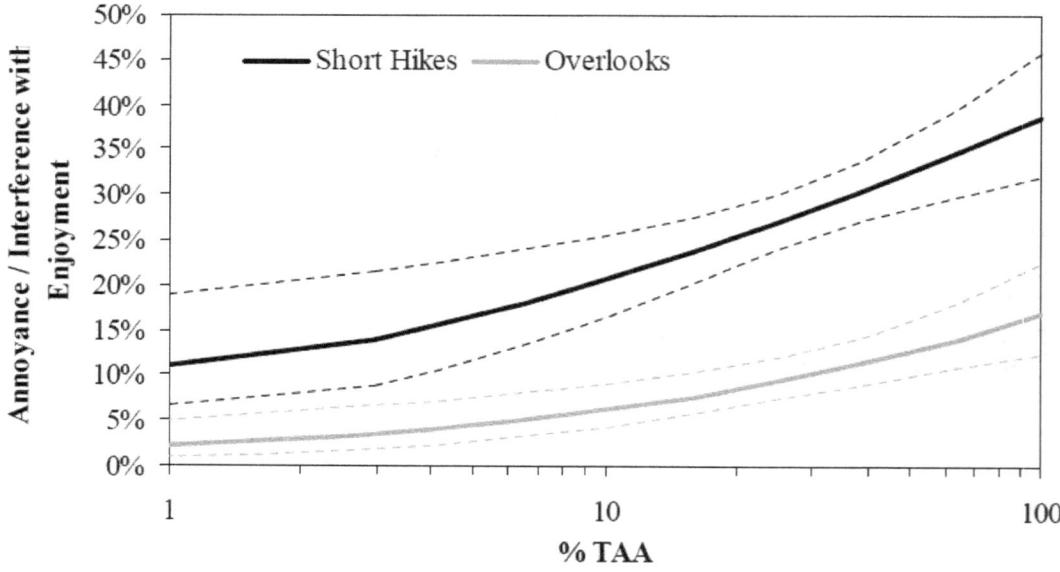

Figure 14. Short Hike and Overlook Dose-Response Curves

Are there other factors, such as age or gender, which influence visitor response to tour aircraft overflight noise?

Yes. It appears that a respondent's familiarity with the site, along with ambient noise level, can influence visitor response to aircraft noise. As shown in Figure 15, six to ten percent more repeat visitors will be annoyed by the same dose of aircraft noise at short hike sites, while one to nine percent more visitors will be annoyed by the same dose of aircraft noise at overlooks. This increased annoyance is a function of dose, with the largest increases being associated with the largest dose. Based on these results the first visit variable was used as a covariate in all of the final dose-response regressions presented in Appendix D.

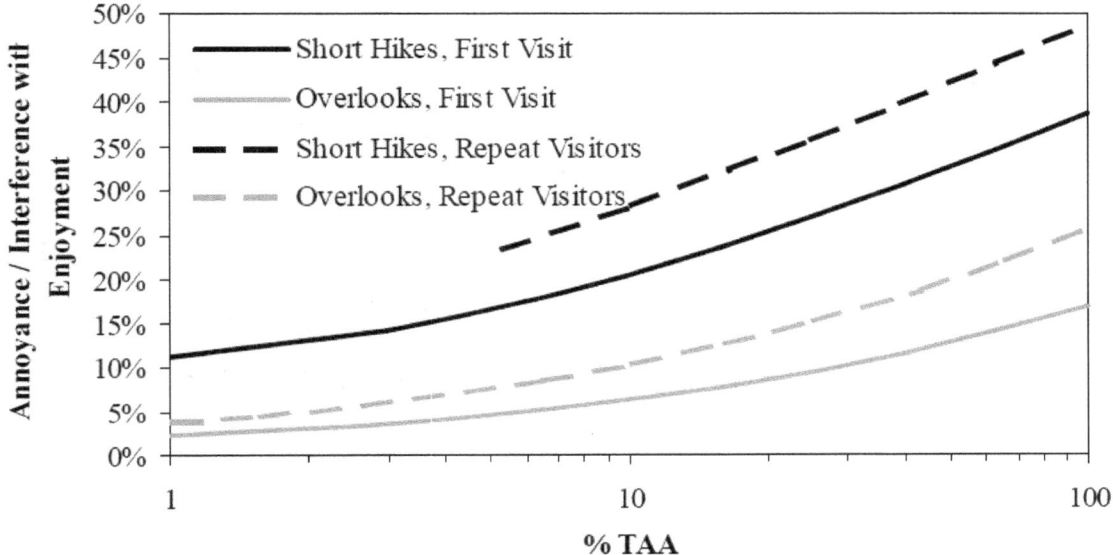

Figure 15. First Time vs. Repeat Visitor Dose-Response Curves

Although there is a significant difference between first time and repeat visitors, the complexity of incorporating this type of information into practical implementation could be prohibitive. For example, how would a park keep track of the population of visitors that were considered repeats?

Additionally, supplementary analysis has shown that ambient noise level and reasons for visit, such as to enjoy the natural quiet or historical significance, can affect visitor response. Factors such as number of people and number of children in the group may have slight influences, but are not significant enough to warrant further study.

Does visitor response to tour aircraft overflight noise at the same location change over time?

An analysis of data from the Point Imperial Overlook at Grand Canyon showed no significant difference in the relationship between acoustic dose and visitor response

Environmental Measurement and Modeling Division
Volpe Center Acoustics Facility
Study of Visitor Response to Air Tour and Other Aircraft Noise in National Parks

January 2005

between the years 1992 and 1999. Because this type of analysis could only be performed for one study location, these results should be considered somewhat preliminary. At the same time, they do represent the best available information. Figure 16 shows the associated dose-response relationships.

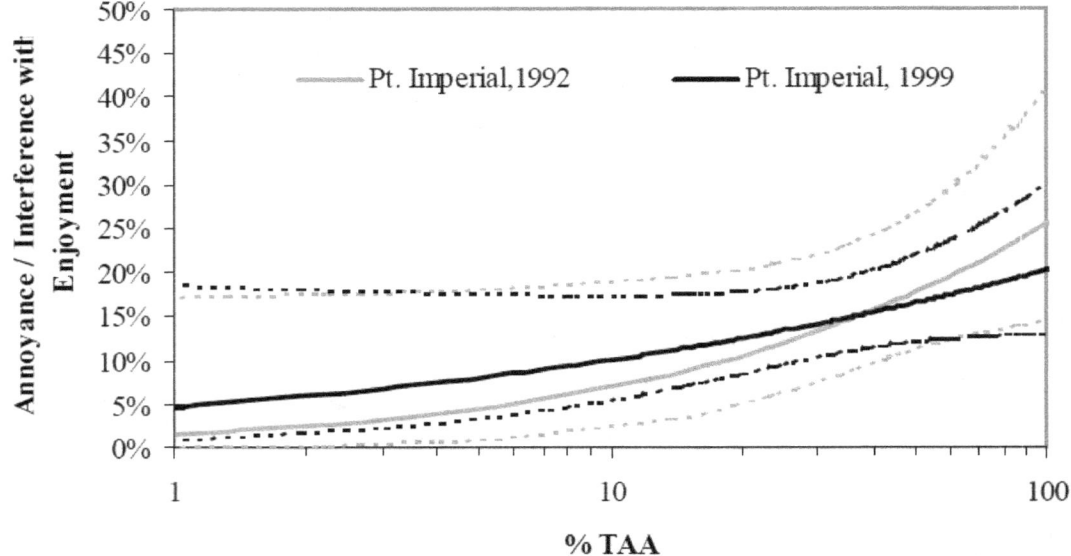

Figure 16. Dose-Response Curves at Point Imperial, 1992 and 1999

4.0 APPLICATION OF DOSE-RESPONSE RELATIONSHIPS

Although the dose-response concept using a single descriptor such as %TAA could be used in a National Park environment, combining two acoustic descriptors may provide added value. This approach would: (1) provide for a more complete assessment of visitor annoyance / interference with enjoyment; and (2) allow for the use of both a level-based acoustic descriptor and a time-based acoustic descriptor.

Intuitively, a single descriptor may not be appropriate in all situations. For example, tour aircraft flying continuously but generating a relatively low sound level would have a high %TAA and a low change in exposure. In this case, using $\Delta L_{AE,Tac}$ alone would provide a less complete assessment of noise. On the other hand, using %TAA for assessment in an environment where there are sparse but extremely loud events (low %TAA and high $\Delta L_{AE,Tac}$) would also result in a less complete assessment. The Pearson Correlations shown in Table 10 and Table 11 back this intuition. It shows that, in most cases, the correlation between the time-based and level-based descriptors is low, indicating that the inclusion of both of these descriptor types would strengthen an impact assessment methodology.

Table 10. Pearson Correlations, Overlooks

	%TA	TAA	%TAA	$L_{Aeq,Tresp}$	$L_{Aeq,1h}$	$\Delta L_{AE,Tac}$	$\Delta L_{AE,Tresp}$	NUMac
%TA	1.00	0.37	0.75	-0.21	-0.13	0.58	0.76	0.69
TAA		1.00	0.81	0.15	0.49	0.86	0.76	0.42
%TAA			1.00	0.11	-0.29	0.13	0.37	0.48
$L_{Aeq,Tresp}$				1.00	0.89	0.29	0.22	0.03
$L_{Aeq,1h}$					1.00	0.59	0.56	0.22
$\Delta L_{AE,Tac}$						1.00	0.84	0.40
$\Delta L_{AE,Tresp}$							1.00	0.56
NUMac								1.00

Table 11. Pearson Correlations, Short Hikes

	%TA	TAA	%TAA	$L_{Aeq,Tresp}$	$L_{Aeq,1h}$	$\Delta L_{AE,Tac}$	$\Delta L_{AE,Tresp}$	NUMac
%TA	1.00	0.31	0.62	0.36	0.29	-0.06	0.41	0.41
TAA		1.00	0.58	0.09	0.24	0.26	0.39	0.61
%TAA			1.00	0.20	0.12	0.40	0.68	0.09
$L_{Aeq,Tresp}$				1.00	0.96	0.51	0.60	0.12
$L_{Aeq,1h}$					1.00	0.48	0.53	0.30
$\Delta L_{AE,Tac}$						1.00	0.87	-0.20
$\Delta L_{AE,Tresp}$							1.00	-0.01
NUMac								1.00

It is anticipated that using one time-based and one level-based descriptor to combine both the temporal quality and level of the noise dose would result in the most complete assessment of noise impact. These acoustic descriptors could be combined by determining their respective values at equal levels of percent annoyance/interference with enjoyment. See Figure 17 as an example, relating the %TAA and $\Delta L_{AE,Tac}$ acoustic descriptors to specific annoyance levels. This graphic shows that it is possible to reduce annoyance by reducing either %TAA or $\Delta L_{AE,Tac}$.

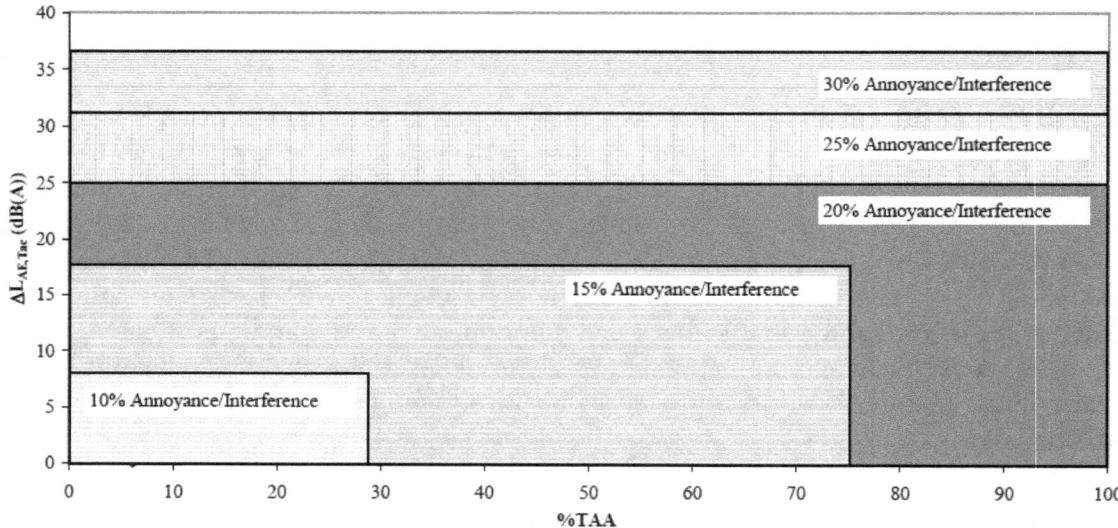

**Figure 17. Example Equal Annoyance Assessment
Overlooks using Top 3 Responses**

Environmental Measurement and Modeling Division
Volpe Center Acoustics Facility   *January 2005*
Study of Visitor Response to Air Tour and Other Aircraft Noise in National Parks

5.0 REFERENCES

1 Fleming, et. al., <u>Development of Noise Dose / Visitor Response Relationships for the National Parks Overflight Rule: Bryce Canyon National Park Study</u>. Washington D.C.: Federal Aviation Administration, July 1998.

2 Rapoza, et.al., "Development of Noise Dose / Visitor Response Relationships at Front-Country Overlook Sites: Bryce and Grand Canyon National Parks," Cambridge, MA: John A Volpe National Transportations Systems Center Acoustics Facility, January 2001.

3 Anderson, et.al., <u>Dose-Response Relationships Derived From Data Collected at Grand Canyon, Haleakala and Hawaii Volcanoes National Parks</u>, NPOA Report No. 93-6, National Park Service, Denver Colorado 80225, October 1993.

4 Schultz, T.J., "Synthesis of social surveys on noise annoyance" J. Acoustical Society of America. Vol 64, p.377-405. August 1978.

5 <u>Electronic Statistics Textbook and Glossary</u>, StatSoft, Inc., STATISTICA (data analysis software system), version 6, 2001.

6 Fields, James M., "Reactions to environmental noise in an ambient noise context in residential areas" J. Acoustical Society of America. Vol 104. p 2245-2260. October 1998.

7 Collett, David, <u>Modeling Binary Data</u>, Second Edition, Chapman & Hall / CRC, London, 2003.

Appendix A

Analysis of Data Collected at Pima Trail and Hermit Basin

Two of the short hike sites at GCNP, Pima Trail and Hermit Basin, were eliminated from analysis due to extenuating factors. These factors included a small number of visitor responses (<35), a limited range of acoustic dose, and an uncertainty of site type. Because of this, individual dose response regressions could not be calculated and the site comparisons in Section 2 could not be conducted for these data sets. These data can, however, be plotted against the final dose-response regressions for short hikes to see if any similarities exist.

Pima Trail was a frontcountry, short hike site, which allowed visitors to travel a short distance along the rim of the canyon from the Pima Point overlook. Although originally classified as a short hike site, it was somewhat unlike the other short hike sites in that the trail followed the rim and was much more susceptible to the non-natural sound unique to a rim site, e.g., automobiles, buses, and a higher density of visitors. There were only 31 visitor responses collected at this site, and the time audible data ranged between 90% and 100%, while the level-based descriptors could not be calculated due to the lack of ambient data, further exemplifying the uniqueness of this site. As a result, dose-response regressions could not be calculated. Figure A-1 shows the average annoyance (using the top 3 dichotomization) and corresponding 95% confidence interval of the data from Pima Trail along with the short hike and overlook regressions.

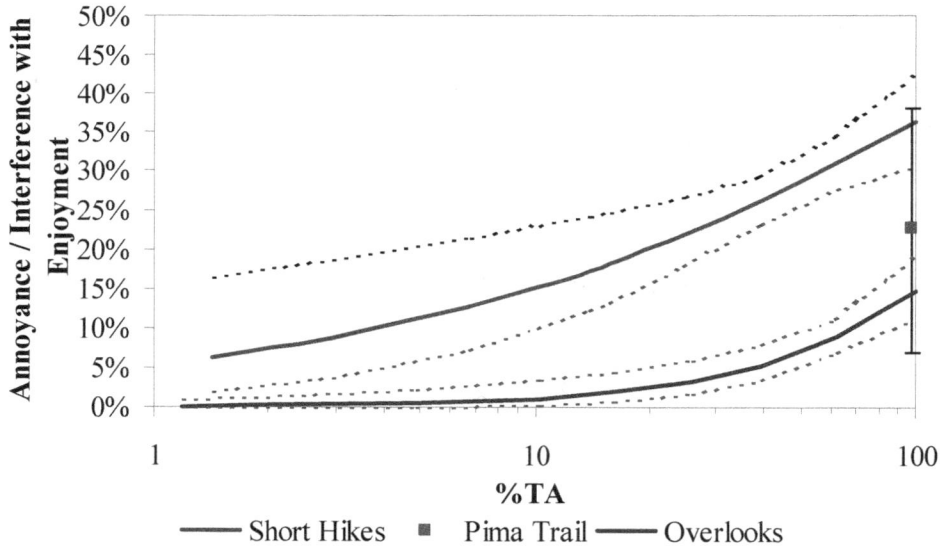

Figure A-1. Average Responses from Pima Trail

This graphic shows that the responses from Pima Trail fall between the short hike and overlook regressions, confirming that it may not be quite similar to either site type.

Hermit Basin was a *backcountry*, short hike site. Because the other short hikes sites were classified as frontcountry sites, it was unclear if this site should be included in the current pool of short hike data. There were only 32 visitor responses collected at this site, and the time audible data ranged between 60% and 100%. Figure A-2 shows the average annoyance (using the top 3 dichotomization) and corresponding 95% confidence interval of the data from Hermit Basin along with the short hike regression.

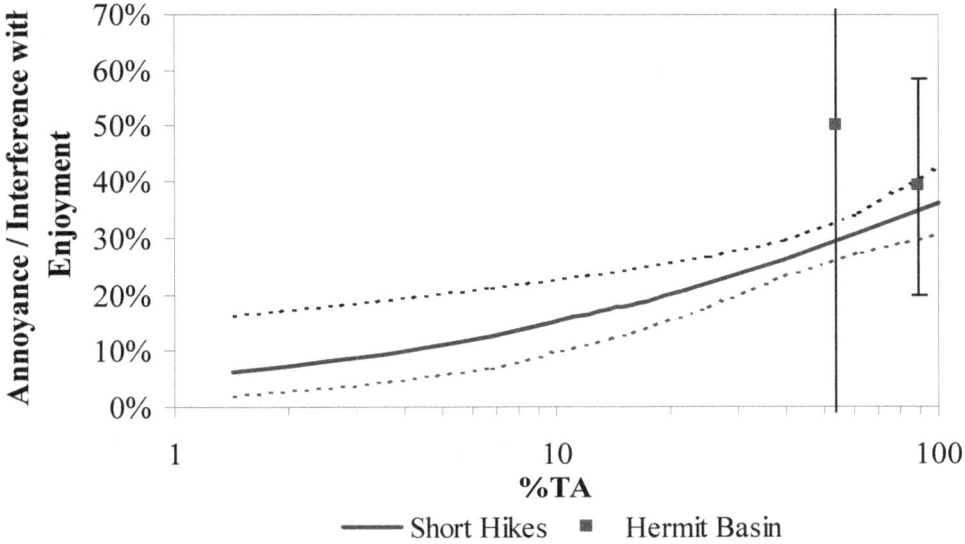

Figure A-2. Average Responses from Hermit Basin

This graphic shows that the average responses from hermit basin are slightly higher than the short hike regression, although the uppermost point is within the confidence limits. Because of the limited number of data points and limited range, no conclusions on the similarity of this site to frontcountry short hikes can be made.

Appendix B:
Summary of Responses to Pertinent Survey Questions

Q3A. Have you ever been to [Sitename] before?

Response	All Short Hikes		Queens Garden		Queens Garden Extended		Haleakala		Wahauala	
	#	%	#	%	#	%	#	%	#	%
No	1112	84.7	450	87.5	333	85.2	175	82.2	154	79.0
Yes	196	14.9	61	11.9	58	14.8	38	17.8	39	20.0
No Response	5	0.4	3	0.6	0	0.0	0	0.0	2	1.0
Total	1313	100.0	514	100.0	391	100.0	213	100.0	195	100.0

Response	All Overlooks		Rainbow Point		Fairyland		Point Imperial		Bryce Point		Pima Point		Lipan Point	
	#	%	#	%	#	%	#	%	#	%	#	%	#	%
No	857	86.6	49	84.5	124	89.3	369	91.1	30	69.8	138	85.2	147	80.3
Yes	123	12.4	9	15.5	13	9.3	33	8.2	11	25.6	23	14.2	34	18.6
No Response	10	1.0	0	0	2	1.4	3	0.7	2	4.7	1	0.6	2	1.1
Total	990	100.0	58	100.0	139	100.0	405	100.0	43	100.0	162	100.0	183	100.0

Q3B. For those who have been to [Sitename] before, about how many times have you visited this site in the past 5 years?

Response	All Short Hikes		Queens Garden		Queens Garden Extended		Haleakala		Wahauala	
	#	%	#	%	#	%	#	%	#	%
0	20	15.3	14	23.0	15	25.9	1	2.6	0	0.0
1	80	40.8	30	49.2	24	41.4	14	36.8	12	30.8
2	43	21.9	13	21.3	11	19.0	1	2.6	18	46.2
3	12	6.1	2	3.3	3	5.2	4	10.5	3	7.7
4	3	1.5	0	0.0	0	0.0	2	5.3	1	2.6
5	4	2.0	1	1.6	0	0.0	2	5.3	1	2.6
6	2	1.0	0	0.0	0	0.0	2	5.3	0	0.0
7	1	0.5	1	1.6	0	0.0	0	0.0	0	0.0
8	1	0.5	0	0.0	0	0.0	1	2.6	0	0.0
10	6	3.1	0	0.0	1	1.7	5	13.2	0	0.0
12	2	1.0	0	0.0	0	0.0	2	5.3	0	0.0
15	2	1.0	0	0.0	1	1.7	1	2.6	0	0.0
20	1	0.5	0	0.0	0	0.0	0	0.0	1	2.6
30	1	0.5	0	0.0	0	0.0	1	2.6	0	0.0

	All Short Hikes		Queens Garden		Queens Garden Extended		Haleakala		Wahauala	
No Response	8	4.1	0	0.0	3	5.2	2	5.3	3	7.7
Total	196	100.0	61	100.0	58	100.0	38	100.0	39	100.0

Response	All Overlooks		Rainbow Point		Fairyland		Point Imperial		Bryce Point		Pima Point		Lipan Point	
	#	%	#	%	#	%	#	%	#	%	#	%	#	%
0	32	26.0	2	22.2	6	46.2	6	18.2	1	9.1	7	30.4	10	29.4
1	38	30.9	3	33.3	2	15.4	12	36.36	5	45.5	7	30.4	9	26.5
2	25	20.3	1	11.1	3	23.1	8	24.24	1	9.1	4	17.4	8	23.5
3	8	6.5	0	0.0	1	7.7	3	9.1	0	0.0	1	4.4	3	8.8
4	5	4.1	0	0.0	1	7.7	2	6.1	1	9.1	1	4.4	0	0.0
6	2	1.6	2	22.2	0	0.0	0	0.0	0	0.0	0	0.0	0	0.0
12	1	0.8	0	0	0	0.0	0	0.0	0	0.0	1	4.35	0	0.0
No Response	12	9.8	1	11.1	0	0.0	2	6.1	3	27.3	2	8.7	4	11.8
Total	123	100.0	9	100.0	13	100.0	33	100.0	11	100.0	23	100.0	34	100.0

Q7A. How important was viewing the natural scenery as a reason for your visit to [Sitename]?

Response	All Short Hikes		Queens Garden		Queens Garden Extended		Haleakala		Wahauala	
	#	%	#	%	#	%	#	%	#	%
Not at all Important	5	0.4	0	0.0	3	0.8	2	0.9	0	0.0
Slightly Important	6	0.5	2	0.4	0	0.0	0	0.0	4	2.1
Moderately Important	54	4.11	15	2.9	15	3.8	8	3.8	16	8.2
Very Important	444	33.8	148	28.8	134	34.3	71	33.3	91	46.7
Extremely Important	800	60.9	349	67.9	236	60.4	131	61.5	84	43.1
No Response	4	0.3	0	0.0	3	0.8	1	0.5	0	0.0
Total	1313	100.0	514	100.0	391	100.0	213	100.0	195	100.0

Environmental Measurement and Modeling Division
Volpe Center Acoustics Facility   January 2005
Study of Visitor Response to Air Tour and Other Aircraft Noise in National Parks

Response	All Overlooks		Rainbow Point		Fairyland		Point Imperial		Bryce Point		Pima Point		Lipan Point	
	#	%	#	%	#	%	#	%	#	%	#	%	#	%
Not at all Important	4	0.4	0	0.0	1	0.7	1	0.3	1	2.3	0	0.0	1	0.6
Slightly Important	3	0.3	0	0.0	1	0.7	1	0.3	0	0.0	1	0.6	0	0.0
Moderately Important	58	5.9	3	5.2	9	6.4	20	4.9	3	7.0	16	9.9	7	3.8
Very Important	320	32.3	23	39.7	54	38.6	120	30.6	13	30.2	64	39.5	42	23.0
Extremely Important	600	60.6	30	51.7	74	53.6	258	63.7	26	60.5	79	48.8	133	72.7
No Response	5	0.5	2	3.5	0	0.0	1	0.2	0	0.0	2	1.2	0	0.0
Total	990	100.0	58	100.0	139	100.0	405	100.0	43	100.0	162	100.0	183	100.0

Q7B. How important was enjoying the natural quiet and sounds of nature as a reason for your visit to [Sitename]?

Response	All Short Hikes		Queens Garden		Queens Garden Extended		Haleakala		Wahauala	
	#	%	#	%	#	%	#	%	#	%
Not at all Important	38	2.9	10	1.9	12	3.1	4	1.9	12	6.1
Slightly Important	121	9.2	48	9.3	33	8.4	13	6.1	27	13.9
Moderately Important	288	21.9	108	21.0	96	24.6	39	18.3	45	23.1
Very Important	469	35.7	181	35.2	160	40.9	67	31.5	61	31.3
Extremely Important	389	29.6	163	31.7	87	22.3	89	41.8	50	25.6
No Response	8	0.6	4	0.8	3	0.8	1	0.5	0	0.0
Total	1313	100.0	514	100.0	391	100.0	213	100.0	195	100.0

Response	All Overlooks		Rainbow Point		Fairyland		Point Imperial		Bryce Point		Pima Point		Lipan Point	
	#	%	#	%	#	%	#	%	#	%	#	%	#	%
Not at all Important	28	2.8	0	0.0	4	2.9	7	1.7	2	4.7	6	3.7	9	4.9
Slightly Important	99	10.0	7	12.1	13	9.3	44	10.9	5	11.6	17	10.5	13	17.1
Moderately Important	228	23.0	13	22.4	33	23.6	78	19.3	13	30.2	45	27.8	46	25.1
Very Important	320	32.3	21	36.2	48	34.3	130	32.1	16	37.2	54	33.3	51	27.9
Extremely Important	307	31.1	17	29.4	40	29.3	144	35.6	7	16.3	36	22.2	63	34.4

	All Overlooks		Rainbow Point		Fairyland		Point Imperial		Bryce Point		Pima Point		Lipan Point	
No Response	8	0.8	0	0.0	1	0.7	2	0.5	0	0.0	4	2.5	1	0.6
Total	990	100.0	58	100.0	139	100.0	405	100.0	43	100.0	162	100.0	183	100.0

Q7C. How important was appreciating the history and cultural significance of the site as a reason for your visit to [Sitename]?

Response	All Short Hikes		Queens Garden		Queens Garden Extended		Haleakala		Wahauala	
	#	%	#	%	#	%	#	%	#	%
Not at all Important	71	5.4	29	5.6	32	8.2	8	3.8	2	1.0
Slightly Important	226	17.2	93	18.1	79	20.2	35	16.4	19	9.7
Moderately Important	426	32.4	193	37.5	141	36.1	51	23.9	41	21.0
Very Important	359	27.3	139	27.0	88	22.5	68	31.9	64	32.8
Extremely Important	223	17.0	57	11.1	49	12.5	50	23.5	67	34.4
No Response	8	0.6	3	0.6	2	0.5	1	0.5	2	1.0
Total	1313	100.0	514	100.0	391	100.0	213	100.0	195	100.0

Response	All Overlooks		Rainbow Point		Fairyland		Point Imperial		Bryce Point		Pima Point		Lipan Point	
	#	%	#	%	#	%	#	%	#	%	#	%	#	%
Not at all Important	57	5.8	4	6.9	7	5.0	29	7.2	2	4.7	6	3.7	9	4.9
Slightly Important	138	13.9	11	19.0	22	15.7	63	15.6	3	7.0	19	11.7	20	10.9
Moderately Important	309	31.3	18	31.0	49	35.7	129	31.9	16	37.2	48	29.6	49	26.8
Very Important	254	25.6	11	19.0	37	26.4	99	24.4	14	32.6	47	29.0	46	25.1
Extremely Important	224	22.6	14	24.1	24	17.1	84	20.7	8	18.6	38	23.5	56	30.6
No Response	8	0.8	0	0.0	0	0.0	1	0.2	0	0.0	4	2.5	3	1.6
Total	990	100.0	58	100.0	139	100.0	405	100.0	43	100.0	162	100.0	183	100.0

Q8.   Did you hear any airplanes, jets, helicopters, or any other aircraft during your visit to [Sitename]?

Response	All Short Hikes		Queens Garden		Queens Garden Extended		Haleakala		Wahauala	
	#	%	#	%	#	%	#	%	#	%
No	322	24.5	128	24.9	131	33.5	55	25.8	8	4.1
Yes	991	75.5	386	75.1	260	66.5	158	74.2	187	95.9
No Response	0	0.0	0	0.0	0.0	0.0	0	0.0	0	0.0
Total	1313	100.0	514	100.0	391	100.0	213	100.0	195	100.0

Response	All Overlooks		Rainbow Point		Fairyland		Point Imperial		Bryce Point		Pima Point		Lipan Point	
	#	%	#	%	#	%	#	%	#	%	#	%	#	%
No	609	61.5	53	91.4	106	75.7	186	45.9	13	30.2	120	74.1	131	71.6
Yes	381	38.4	5	8.6	33	23.6	219	54.1	30	69.8	42	25.9	52	28.4
Total	990	100.0	58	100.0	139	100.0	405	100.0	43	100.0	162	100.0	183	100.0

Q9.   Were you bothered or annoyed by aircraft noise during your visit to [Sitename]?

Response	All Short Hikes		Queens Garden		Queens Garden Extended		Haleakala		Wahauala	
	#	%	#	%	#	%	#	%	#	%
No AC Heard	322	24.5	128	24.9	131	33.5	55	25.8	8	4.1
Not at all Annoyed	265	26.7	95	24.6	53	20.4	39	24.7	78	41.7
Slightly Annoyed	263	26.5	87	22.5	60	23.1	49	31.0	67	35.8
Moderately Annoyed	182	18.4	69	17.9	53	20.4	35	22.2	25	13.4
Very Annoyed	80	8.1	38	9.8	18	6.9	16	10.1	8	4.3
Extremely Annoyed	75	7.6	33	8.5	14	5.4	19	12.0	9	4.8
No Response	126	12.7	64	16.6	62	23.8	0	0.0	0	0.0
Total	1313	100.0	514	100.0	391	100.0	213	100.0	195	100.0

Response	All Overlooks		Rainbow Point		Fairyland		Point Imperial		Bryce Point		Pima Point		Lipan Point	
	#	%	#	%	#	%	#	%	#	%	#	%	#	%
No AC Heard	609	61.5	53	91.4	106	75.7	186	45.9	13	30.2	120	74.1	131	71.6
Not at all Annoyed	190	49.9	4	80.0	11	33.3	96	43.8	19	63.4	27	64.3	33	63.5

	All Overlooks		Rainbow Point		Fairyland		Point Imperial		Bryce Point		Pima Point		Lipan Point	
Slightly Annoyed	95	24.9	0	0.0	10	30.3	63	28.8	4	13.3	7	16.6	11	21.2
Moderately Annoyed	69	18.1	1	20.0	9	27.3	45	20.6	6	20.0	5	11.9	3	5.8
Very Annoyed	14	3.7	0	0.0	3	9.1	6	2.7	1	3.3	2	4.8	2	3.9
Extremely Annoyed	10	2.6	0	0.0	0	0.0	8	3.7	0	0.0	0	0.0	2	3.9
No Response	3	0.8	0	0.0	0	0.0	1	0.5	0	0.0	1	2.4	1	1.9
Total	990	100.0	58	100.0	139	100.0	405	100.0	43	100.0	162	100.0	183	100.0

Q10A. How much did the sound from aircraft interfere with each of the following aspects of your visit at [Sitename]?

Enjoyment of the site

Response	All Short Hikes		Queens Garden		Queens Garden Extended		Haleakala		Wahauala	
	#	%	#	%	#	%	#	%	#	%
No AC Heard	322	24.5	128	24.9	131	33.5	55	25.8	8	4.1
Not at all	346	34.9	132	34.2	71	27.3	53	33.5	90	48.1
Slightly	220	22.2	74	19.2	54	20.8	43	27.2	49	26.2
Moderately	168	17.0	60	15.5	50	19.2	31	19.6	27	14.4
Very Much	84	8.5	35	9.1	13	5.0	19	12.0	17	9.1
Extremely	40	4.0	15	3.9	9	3.5	12	7.6	4	2.1
No Response	132	13.4	70	18.1	63	24.2	0	0.0	0	0.0
Total	1313	100.0	514	100.0	391	100.0	213	100.0	195	100.0

Response	All Overlooks		Rainbow Point		Fairyland		Point Imperial		Bryce Point		Pima Point		Lipan Point	
	#	%	#	%	#	%	#	%	#	%	#	%	#	%
No AC Heard	609	61.5	53	91.4	106	75.7	186	45.9	13	30.2	120	74.1	131	71.6
Not at all	202	53.0	3	60.0	14	42.4	106	48.4	18	60.0	30	71.4	31	59.6
Slightly	96	25.2	2	40.0	8	24.2	60	27.4	9	30.0	5	11.9	12	23.1
Moderately	59	15.5	0	0.0	7	21.2	40	18.3	2	6.7	4	9.5	6	11.5
Very Much	15	3.9	0	0.0	4	12.1	9	4.1	1	3.3	1	2.4	0	0.0
Extremely	6	1.6	0	0.0	0	0.0	2	0.9	0	0.0	1	2.4	3	5.8
No Response	3	0.8	0	0.0	0	0.0	2	0.9	0	0.0	1	2.4	0	0.0
Total	990	100.0	58	100.0	139	100.0	405	100.0	43	100.0	162	100.0	183	100.0

Q10B. How much did the sound from aircraft interfere with each of the following aspects of your visit at [Sitename]?

Appreciation of the natural quiet and sound of nature

Response	All Short Hikes		Queens Garden		Queens Garden Extended		Haleakala		Wahauala	
	#	%	#	%	#	%	#	%	#	%
No AC Heard	322	24.5	128	24.9	131	33.5	55	25.8	8	4.1
Not at all	144	14.5	41	10.6	38	14.6	23	14.6	42	22.5
Slightly	224	22.6	92	23.8	44	16.9	36	22.8	52	27.8
Moderately	203	20.5	68	17.6	52	20.0	38	24.1	45	24.1
Very Much	160	16.1	64	16.6	36	13.8	32	20.3	28	15.0
Extremely	125	12.6	48	12.4	28	10.8	29	18.4	20	10.7
No Response	135	13.6	73	18.9	62	23.8	0	0.0	0	0.0
Total	1313	100.0	514	100.0	391	100.0	213	100.0	195	100.0

Response	All Overlooks		Rainbow Point		Fairyland		Point Imperial		Bryce Point		Pima Point		Lipan Point	
	#	%	#	%	#	%	#	%	#	%	#	%	#	%
No AC Heard	609	61.5	53	91.4	106	75.7	186	45.9	13	30.2	120	74.1	131	71.6
Not at all	110	28.9	4	80.0	7	21.2	52	23.7	10	33.3	19	45.2	18	34.6
Slightly	96	25.2	0	0.0	9	27.3	53	24.2	10	33.3	9	21.4	15	28.9
Moderately	73	19.2	1	20.0	2	6.1	49	22.4	7	23.3	5	11.9	9	17.3
Very Much	57	15.0	0	0.0	6	18.2	39	17.8	2	6.7	5	11.9	5	9.6
Extremely	41	10.8	0	0.0	9	27.3	23	10.5	3	3.3	3	7.1	5	9.6
No Response	4	1.0	0	0.0	0	0.0	3	1.4	0	0.0	1	2.4	0	0.0
Total	990	100.0	58	100.0	139	100.0	405	100.0	43	100.0	162	100.0	183	100.0

Q10C. How much did the sound from aircraft interfere with each of the following aspects of your visit at [Sitename]?
Appreciation of the historical and/or cultural significance

Response	All Short Hikes		Queens Garden		Queens Garden Extended		Haleakala		Wahauala	
	#	%	#	%	#	%	#	%	#	%
No AC Heard	322	24.5	128	24.9	131	33.5	55	25.8	8	4.1
Not at all	430	43.3	169	43.8	94	36.2	23	14.6	42	22.5
Slightly	196	19.8	66	17.1	49	18.8	36	22.8	52	27.8
Moderately	127	12.8	42	10.9	34	13.1	38	24.1	45	24.1
Very Much	69	7.0	24	6.2	17	6.5	32	20.3	28	15.0
Extremely	34	3.4	12	3.1	4	1.5	29	18.4	20	10.7
No Response	135	13.6	73	18.9	62	23.8	0	0.0	0	0.0
Total	1313	100.0	514	100.0	391	100.0	213	100.0	195	100.0

Response	All Overlooks		Rainbow Point		Fairyland		Point Imperial		Bryce Point		Pima Point		Lipan Point	
	#	%	#	%	#	%	#	%	#	%	#	%	#	%
No AC Heard	609	61.5	53	91.4	106	75.7	186	45.9	13	30.2	120	74.1	131	71.6
Not at all	236	61.9	4	80.0	19	57.6	129	58.9	18	60.0	29	69.1	37	71.2
Slightly	73	19.2	1	20.0	6	18.2	47	21.5	6	20.0	6	14.3	7	13.5
Moderately	38	10.0	0	0.0	3	9.1	23	10.5	6	20.0	3	7.1	3	5.8
Very Much	16	4.2	0	0.0	4	12.1	9	4.1	0	0.0	1	2.4	0	0.0
Extremely	14	3.7	0	0.0	1	3.0	8	3.7	0	0.0	2	4.8	0	0.0
No Response	4	1.0	0	0.0	0	0	3	1.4	0	0.0	1	2.4	0	0.0
Total	990	100.0	58	100.0	139	100.0	405	100.0	43	100.0	162	100.0	183	100.0

Number of Adults in Group

Response	All Short Hikes		Queens Garden		Queens Garden Extended		Haleakala		Wahauala	
	#	%	#	%	#	%	#	%	#	%
1	92	7.0	39	7.6	25	6.4	13	6.1	15	7.7
2	836	63.7	296	57.6	253	64.7	147	69.0	140	71.8
3	154	11.7	70	13.6	46	11.8	12	5.6	26	13.3

	All Short Hikes		Queens Garden		Queens Garden Extended		Haleakala		Wahauala	
4	133	10.1	79	15.4	25	6.4	15	7.0	14	7.2
5	33	2.5	5	1.0	20	5.1	8	3.8	0	0.0
6	18	1.4	18	3.5	0	0.0	0	0.0	0	0.0
7	12	0.9	0	0.0	0	0.0	12	5.6	0	0.0
9	13	1.0	0	0.0	7	1.8	6	2.8	0	0.0
10	7	0.5	7	1.4	0	0.0	0	0.0	0	0.0
12	1	0.1	0	0.0	1	0.3	0	0.0	0	0.0
14	14	1.1	0	0.0	14	3.6	0	0.0	0	0.0
Total	1313	100.0	514	100.0	391	100.0	213	100.0	195	100.0

Response	All Overlooks		Rainbow Point		Fairyland		Point Imperial		Bryce Point		Pima Point		Lipan Point	
	#	%	#	%	#	%	#	%	#	%	#	%	#	%
1	47	4.7	7	12.1	10	7.1	10	2.5	6	14.0	7	4.3	7	3.8
2	556	56.2	44	75.9	96	69.3	233	57.5	15	34.9	75	46.3	93	50.8
3	134	13.5	0	0.0	14	10.0	55	13.6	9	20.9	23	14.2	33	18.0
4	187	18.9	6	10.3	18	12.9	73	18.0	12	27.9	47	29.0	31	16.9
5	38	3.8	0	0.0	1	0.7	21	5.2	1	2.3	8	4.9	7	3.8
6	8	0.8	1	1.7	0	0.0	0	0.0	0	0.0	0	0.0	7	3.8
7	9	0.9	0	0.0	0	0.0	4	1.0	0	0.0	0	0.0	5	2.7
9	1	0.1	0	0.0	0	0.0	1	0.3	0	0.0	0	0.0	0	0.0
12	2	0.2	0	0.0	0	0.0	0	0.0	0	0.0	2	1.2	0	0.0
14	2	0.2	0	0.0	0	0.0	2	0.5	0	0.0	0	0.0	0	0.0
15	3	0.3	0	0.0	0	0.0	3	0.7	0	0.0	0	0.0	0	0.0
16	2	0.2	0	0.0	0	0.0	2	0.5	0	0.0	0	0.0	0	0.0
45	1	0.1	0	0.0	0	0.0	1	0.3	0	0.0	0	0.0	0	0.0
Total	990	100.0	58	100.0	139	100.0	405	100.0	43	100.0	162	100.0	183	100.0

Number of Children (under 16 years of age) in Group

Response	All Short Hikes		Queens Garden		Queens Garden Extended		Haleakala		Wahauala	
	#	%	#	%	#	%	#	%	#	%
0	1048	79.8	358	69.7	311	79.5	190	89.2	189	96.9
1	131	10.0	65	12.6	41	10.5	19	8.9	6	3.1
2	96	7.3	66	12.8	26	6.7	4	1.9	0	0.0
3	26	2.0	14	2.7	12	3.1	0	0.0	0	0.0
4	1	0.1	0	0.0	1	0.3	0	0.0	0	0.0
5	3	0.2	3	0.6	0	0.0	0	0.0	0	0.0
6	4	0.3	4	0.8	0	0.0	0	0.0	0	0.0
7	4	0.3	4	0.8	0	0.0	0	0.0	0	0.0
Total	1313	100.0	514	100.0	391	100.0	213	100.0	195	100.0

Response	All Overlooks		Rainbow Point		Fairyland		Point Imperial		Bryce Point		Pima Point		Lipan Point	
	#	%	#	%	#	%	#	%	#	%	#	%	#	%
0	663	67.0	37	63.8	82	59.3	284	70.1	30	69.8	97	59.9	133	72.7
1	154	15.5	2	3.5	20	14.3	67	16.5	8	18.6	31	19.1	26	14.2
2	102	10.3	14	24.1	22	15.7	31	7.7	5	11.6	20	12.4	10	5.5
3	58	5.9	4	6.9	12	8.6	17	4.2	0	0.0	11	6.8	14	7.7
4	12	1.2	0	0.0	3	2.1	6	1.5	0	0.0	3	1.9	0	0.0
5	1	0.1	1	1.7	0	0.0	0	0.0	0	0.0	0	0.0	0	0.0
Total	990	100.0	58	100.0	139	100.0	405	100.0	43	100.0	162	100.0	183	100.0

Total number of people in group

Response	All Short Hikes		Queens Garden		Queens Garden Extended		Haleakala		Wahauala	
	#	%	#	%	#	%	#	%	#	%
1	77	5.9	32	6.2	18	4.6	13	6.1	14	7.2
2	695	52.9	196	38.1	220	56.3	140	65.7	139	71.3
3	168	13.0	87	16.9	41	10.5	15	7.0	25	12.8
4	203	15.5	129	25.1	46	11.8	11	5.2	17	8.7
5	64	4.9	25	4.9	31	7.9	8	3.8	0	0.0

	All Short Hikes		Queens Garden		Queens Garden Extended		Haleakala		Wahauala	
6	44	3.4	27	5.3	9	2.3	8	3.8	0	0.0
7	16	1.2	0	0.0	4	1.0	12	5.6	0	0.0
8	3	0.2	3	0.6	0	0.0	0	0.0	0	0.0
9	13	1.0	0	0.0	7	1.8	6	2.8	0	0.0
10	11	0.8	11	2.1	0	0.0	0	0.0	0	0.0
11	4	0.3	4	0.8	0	0.0	0	0.0	0	0.0
12	1	0.1	0	0.0	1	0.3	0	0.0	0	0.0
14	14	1.1	0	0.0	14	3.6	0	0.0	0	0.0
Total	1313	100.0	514	100.0	391	100.0	213	100.0	195	100.0

Response	All Overlooks		Rainbow Point		Fairyland		Point Imperial		Bryce Point		Pima Point		Lipan Point	
	#	%	#	%	#	%	#	%	#	%	#	%	#	%
1	33	3.3	6	10.3	5	3.6	8	1.9	5	11.6	3	1.9	6	3.3
2	398	40.3	26	44.8	62	45.0	180	44.4	10	23.3	48	29.6	72	39.3
3	129	13.0	1	1.7	14	10.0	57	14.1	6	14.0	19	11.7	32	17.5
4	259	26.1	19	32.8	31	22.1	89	22.0	20	46.5	56	34.6	44	24.0
5	86	8.7	3	5.2	24	17.1	22	5.4	1	2.3	22	13.6	14	7.7
6	40	4.0	1	1.7	3	2.1	31	7.7	1	2.3	4	2.5	0	0.0
7	18	1.8	2	3.5	0	0.0	5	1.2	0	0.0	8	4.9	3	1.6
8	5	0.5	0	0.0	0	0.0	0	0.0	0	0.0	0	0.0	5	2.7
9	8	0.8	0	0.0	0	0.0	1	0.3	0	0.0	0	0.0	7	3.8
11	4	0.4	0	0.0	0	0.0	4	1.0	0	0.0	0	0.0	0	0.0
12	2	0.2	0	0.0	0	0.0	0	0.0	0	0.0	2	1.2	0	0.0
14	2	0.2	0	0.0	0	0.0	2	0.5	0	0.0	0	0.0	0	0.0
15	3	0.3	0	0.0	0	0.0	3	0.7	0	0.0	0	0.0	0	0.0
16	2	0.2	0	0.0	0	0.0	2	0.5	0	0.0	0	0.0	0	0.0
45	1	0.1	0	0.0	0	0.0	1	0.3	0	0.0	0	0.0	0	0.0
Total	990	100.0	58	100.0	139	100.0	405	100.0	43	100.0	162	100.0	183	100.0

Gender

Response	All Short Hikes		Queens Garden		Queens Garden Extended		Haleakala		Wahauala	
	#	%	#	%	#	%	#	%	#	%
Male	661	50.3	259	50.4	182	46.5	118	55.4	102	52.3
Female	641	48.8	250	48.6	206	52.7	93	43.7	92	47.2
No Answer	11	0.8	5	1.0	3	0.8	2	0.9	1	0.5
Total	1313	100.0	514	100.0	391	100.0	213	100.0	195	100.0

Response	All Overlooks		Rainbow Point		Fairyland		Point Imperial		Bryce Point		Pima Point		Lipan Point	
	#	%	#	%	#	%	#	%	#	%	#	%	#	%
Male	463	46.7	25	43.1	62	44.3	198	48.9	18	41.9	67	41.4	93	50.8
Female	518	52.3	32	55.2	76	59.0	204	50.4	25	58.1	91	56.2	89	48.6
No Response	10	1.0	0	1.7	1	0.7	3	0.7	0	0.0	4	2.5	1	0.6
Total	990	100.0	58	100.0	139	100.0	405	100.0	43	100.0	162	100.0	183	100.0

Appendix C
Statistical Analysis of Response Dichotomizations

Appendix C presents a summary of the statistical analysis conducted to determine if there is a clear justification for the choice of response dichotomizations.

C.1 Goodness-of-Fit Statistics

Table C-1 shows the Pearson's Chi^2 statistic for overlooks and short hikes[**], for each response dichotomization (top 2, top3, and top 4). The Pearson's Chi^2 statistic gives a reliable measure of the goodness of fit of a particular binary data regression[7]. In performing a relative comparison of scores, a lower number indicates a better fit.

Table C-1. Fit Comparison

Acoustic Descriptor	Response Dichotomization					
	Overlooks			Short Hikes		
	Top 2	Top 3	Top 4	Top 2	Top 3	Top 4
%TA	1.01	1.09	1.06	1.00	1.02	1.00
%TN	1.00	1.01	1.00	1.00	1.00	1.00
TAA	1.01	0.98	0.99	1.00	1.00	1.00
%TAA	1.02	1.09	1.05	1.01	1.01	1.00
$L_{Aeq,Tac}$	1.00	1.00	1.00	1.00	1.00	1.00
$L_{Aeq,Tresp}$	1.01	0.99	1.00	1.00	1.00	1.00
$L_{Aeq,1h}$	1.00	0.97	0.99	1.00	1.01	1.00
$\Delta L_{AE,Tac}$	NA	0.98	0.99	1.00	1.00	1.00
$\Delta L_{AE,Tresp}$	NA	0.99	1.00	1.00	1.00	1.00
L_{Asmx}	1.01	1.00	1.00	1.00	1.00	1.00
NUM_{AC}	NA	0.99	1.00	1.00	1.00	1.00
$NUM_{ac/hr}$	1.01	1.00	1.00	1.00	1.00	1.00

In this Table, the shaded areas show instances where the fit is clearly better (a difference of 0.02 or greater) for a particular dichotomization. In most instances, the statistics are extremely close, and in many cases, equal. For overlooks, the top two dichotomization provides a better fit for %TA and %TAA, while the top 3 dichotomization provides a better fit for $L_{Aeq,1h}$. Neither dichotomization provides for a better fit for the remaining descriptors for overlooks or any of the descriptors for short hikes. Therefore, it is not appropriate to conclude that one dichotomization provides for a better regression fit.

C.2 Model Reliability

Tables C-2 and C-3 explore the model reliability using each response dichotomization for short hikes and overlooks. Reliability is judged by finding the significance of the acoustic descriptors for the original data set and for four bootstrapped data sets for overlooks and short hikes. When a measure was significant at the .05 level, it received a point. Because it was also useful to know when a measure is "powerful" as well as just significant, an additional point was added if the measure is significant at the .001 level.

When combining the results, it is possible for any given descriptor to receive between 0 and 10 points as a measure of overall reliability. If the descriptor scored a total of zero points, it would indicate that the descriptor was never significant at the .05 level for any of the data sets. In the same way, a score of 10 points would indicate that the descriptor

---

[**] Data from short hike sites were culled as summarized in Section 2.3.2.3

was always significant at the .001 level or better. The reliability scores are shown in Table C-2 for overlooks and short hikes.

Table C-2. Reliability Scores for Acoustic Descriptors

Acoustic Descriptor	Reliability Scores					
	Overlooks, top 2	Overlooks, top 3	Overlooks, top 4	Short Hikes, top 2	Short Hikes, top 3	Short Hikes, top 4
%TA	0		7	2	5	4
%TN	0	1	2	2	4	8
TAA	0	10	10	1	6	10
%TAA	0	10	10	4	6	5
$L_{Aeq,Tac}$	0	0	0	2	1	10
$L_{Aeq,Tresp}$	0	3	4	2	1	10
$L_{Aeq,1h}$	0	5	7	2	1	10
$\Delta L_{AE,Tac}$	0	1	9	6	4	10
$\Delta L_{AE,Tresp}$	0	2	7	5	6	10
L_{Asmx}	0	0	0	2	1	10
NUM_{ac}	0	5	3	0	4	1
$NUM_{ac/hr}$	1	1	1	1	0	6

In this Table, shaded cells indicate where the reliability score is highest for a particular descriptor. It shows that the top four dichotomization is most reliable for the level-based descriptors, while the top three is most reliable for the majority of the time-based and number based descriptors. Also worthy of note is that, when using the top two dichotomization for overlooks, the coefficient of the acoustic descriptor almost never achieves a 5% significance level. This is due to the low occurrence of highly annoyed respondents, which results in an essentially 'flat' dose-response curve.

When goodness-of-fit and reliability are considered together, no one dichotomization can be said to perform well in both tests.

Appendix D:
Dose Response Curves

Appendix D contains the dose-response curves for the eight best performing acoustic descriptors for both overlooks and short hikes. These curves are applicable for first-time visitors only. Response curves for repeat visitors can be found by evaluating the equation in Section 2.4 using the coefficients listed in Appendix F.

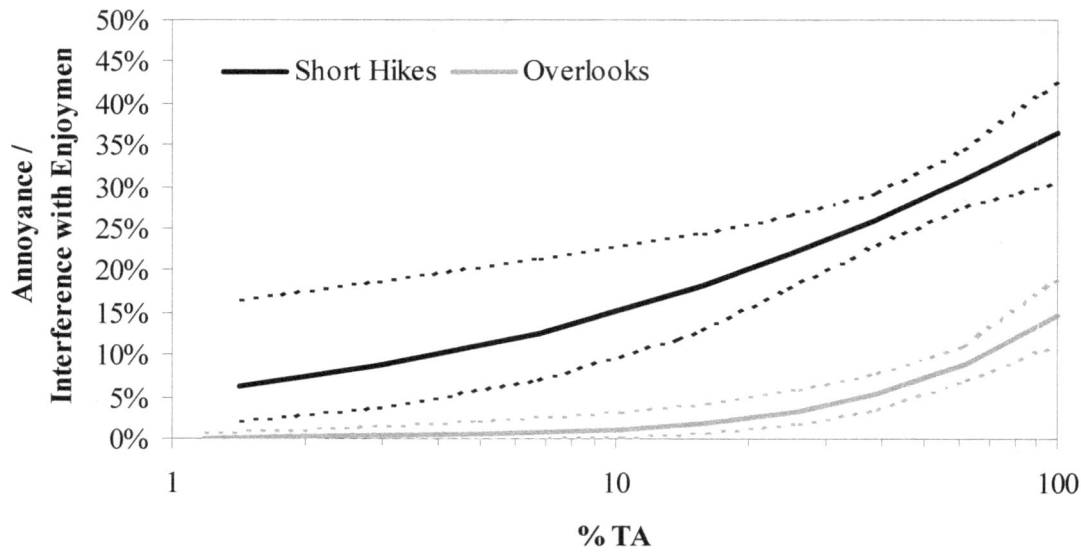

**Figure D-1. Annoyance Dose-Response Curves, Percent Time Audible (%TA)
(Top 3)**

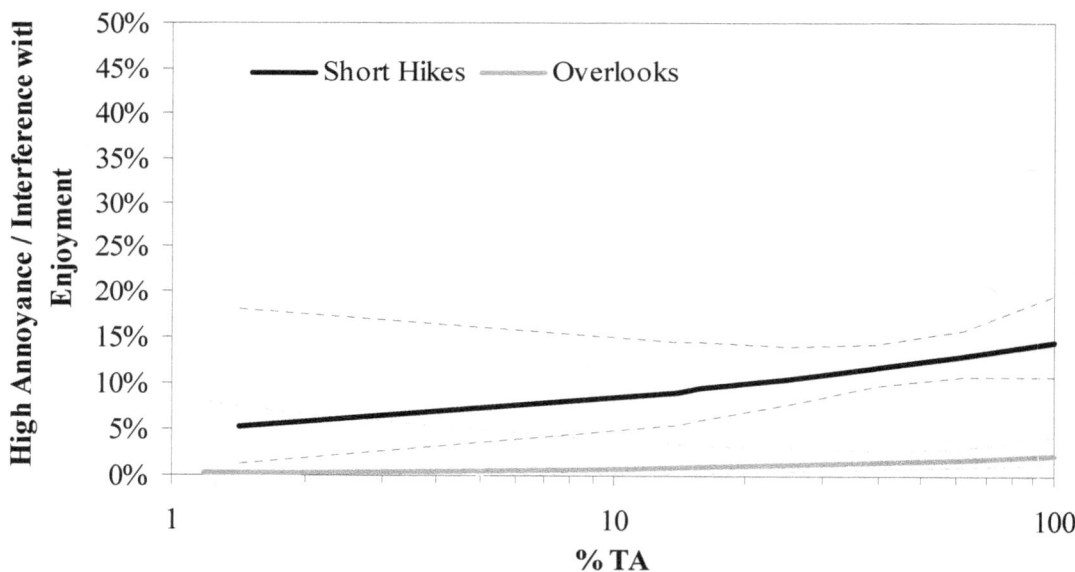

**Figure D-2. High Annoyance Dose-Response Curves, Percent Time Audible (%TA)
(Top 2)**

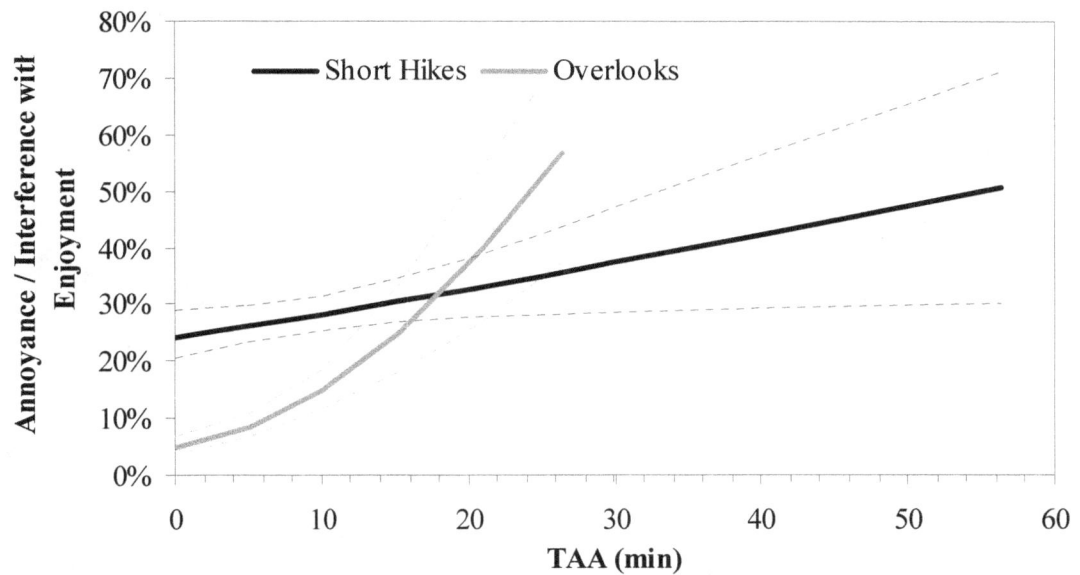

Figure D-3. Dose-Response Curves, Time Above Ambient (TAA) (Top 3)

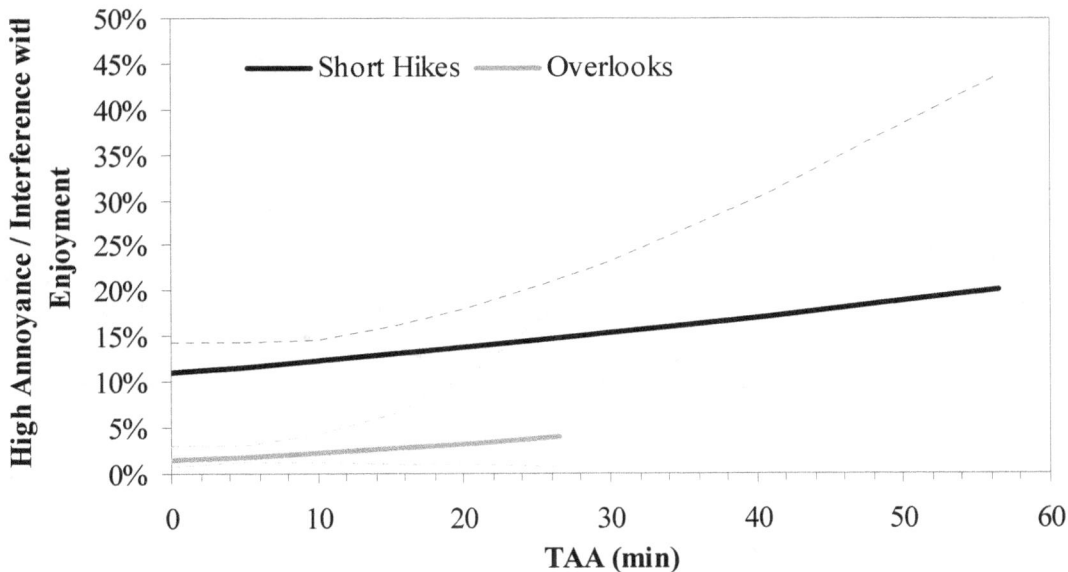

Figure D-4. High Annoyance Dose-Response Curves, Time Above Ambient (TAA) (Top 2)

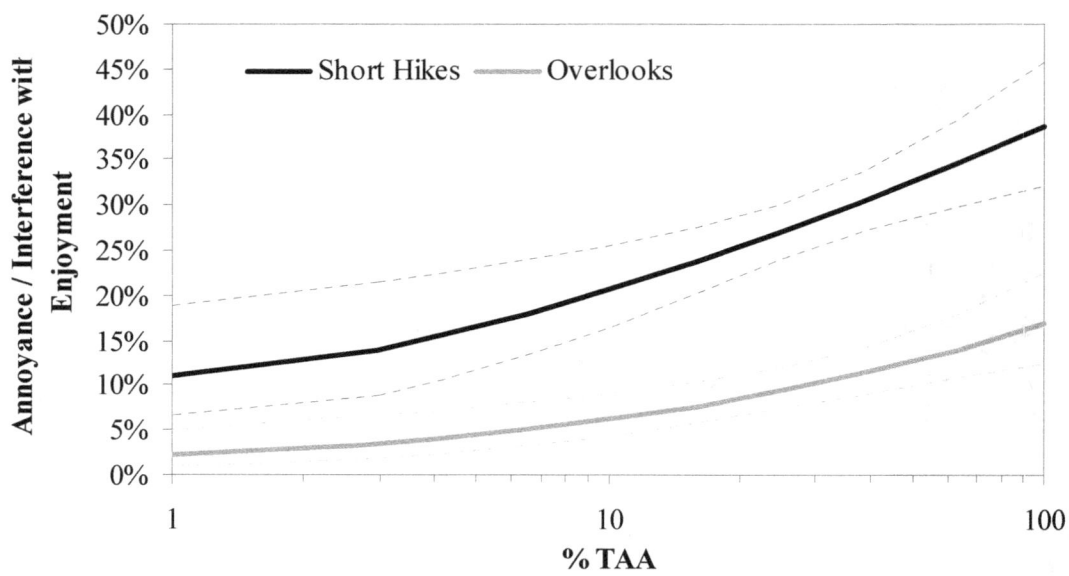

Figure D-5. Dose-Response Curves, % Time Above Ambient (%TAA) (Top 3)

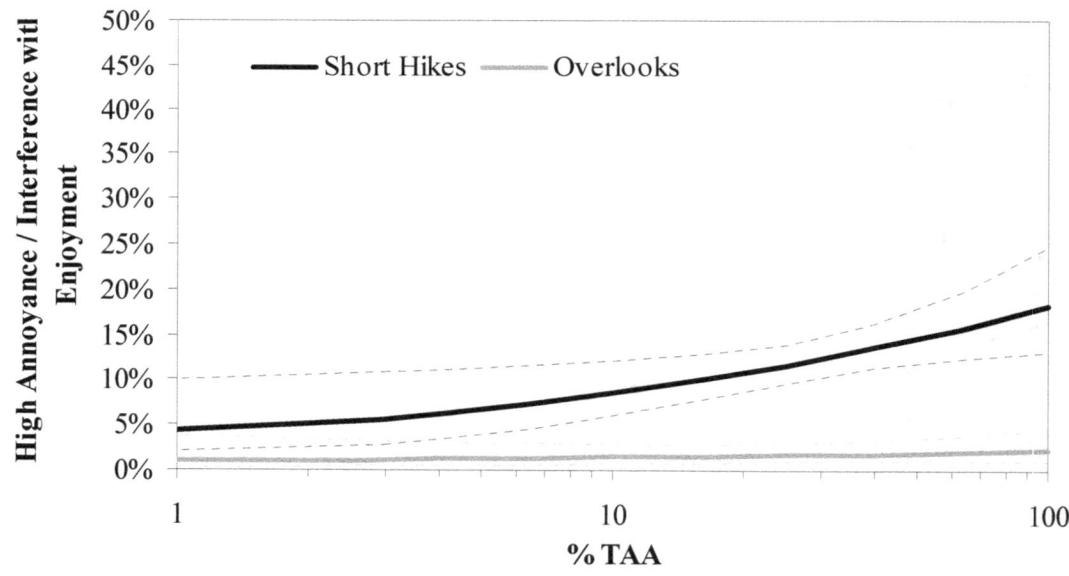

Figure D-6. High Annoyance Dose-Response Curves, % Time Above Ambient (%TAA) (Top 2)

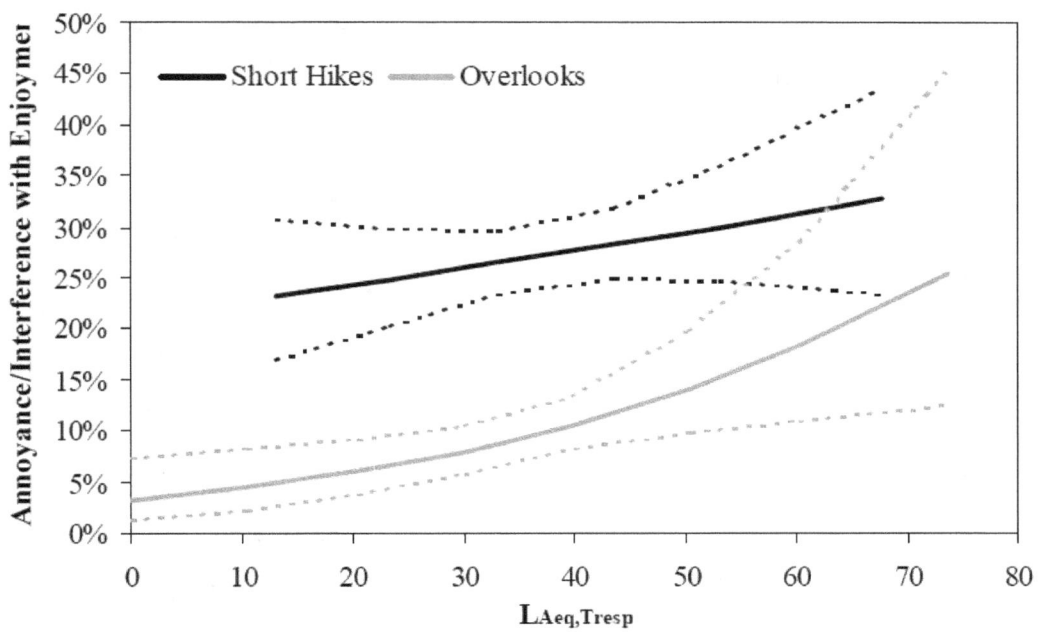

Figure D-7. Annoyance Dose-Response Curves, Aircraft Equivalent Sound Level Normalized to the Respondent's Duration (L$_{Aeq,Tresp}$) (Top 3)

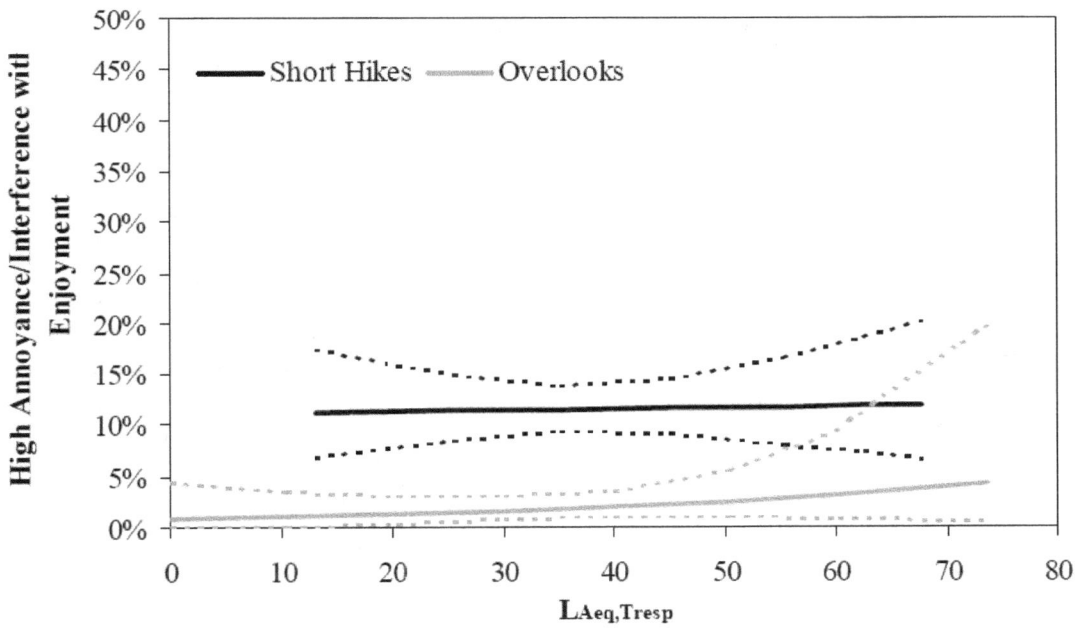

Figure D-8. High Annoyance Dose-Response Curves, Aircraft Equivalent Sound Level Normalized to the Respondent's Duration (L$_{Aeq,Tresp}$) (Top 2)

Environmental Measurement and Modeling Division
Volpe Center Acoustics Facility   *January 2005*
    Study of Visitor Response to Air Tour and Other Aircraft Noise in National Parks

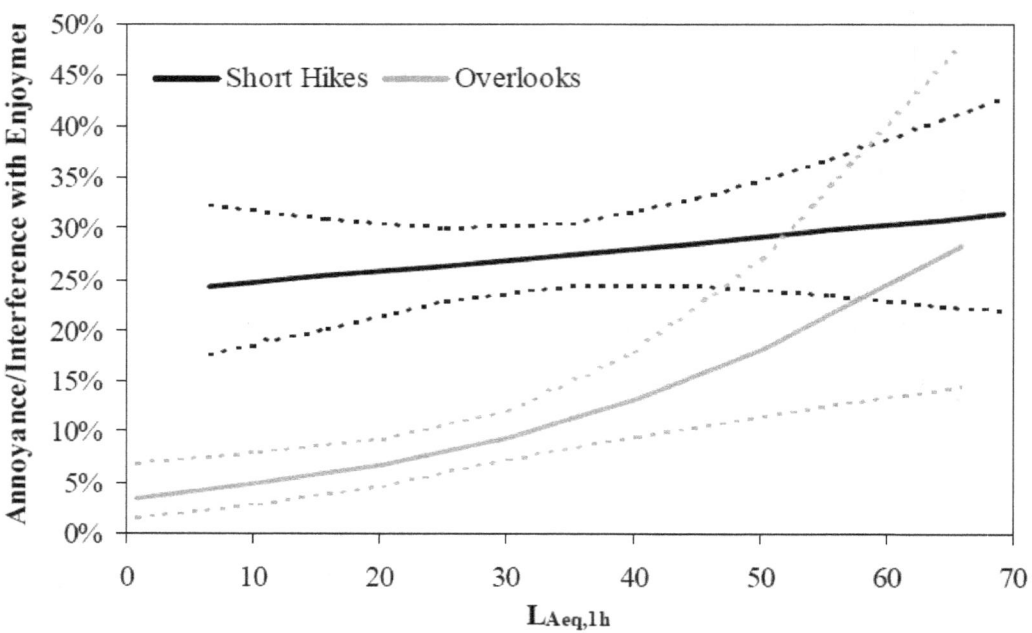

Figure D-9. Annoyance Dose-Response Curves, Aircraft Equivalent Sound Level Normalized to a One-Hour Time Period ($L_{Aeq,1h}$) (Top 3)

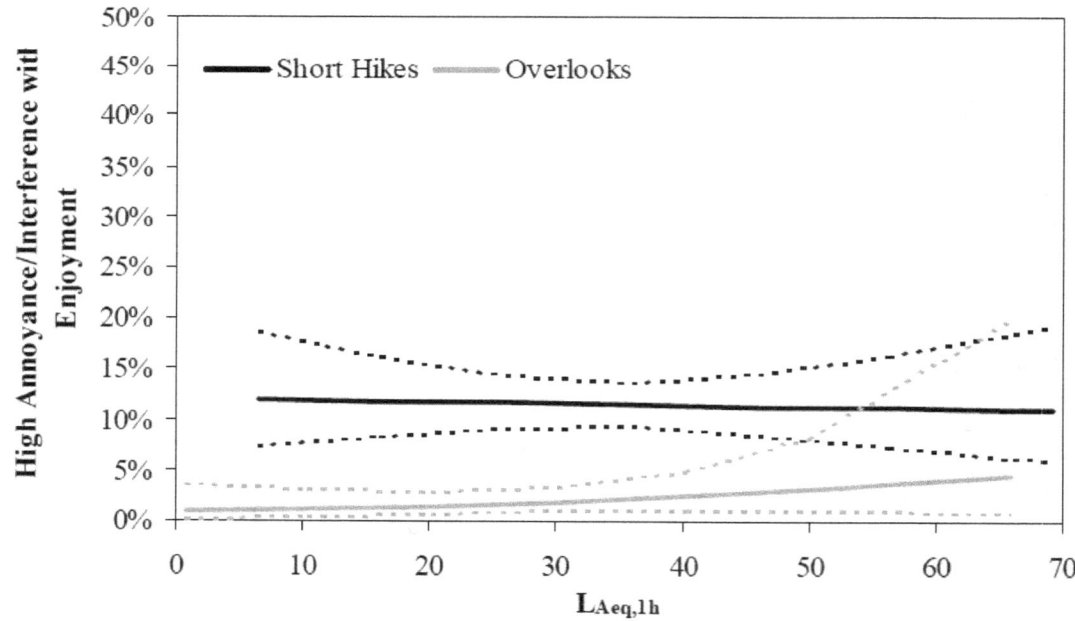

Figure D-10. High Annoyance Dose-Response Curves, Aircraft Equivalent Sound Level Normalized to a One-Hour Time Period ($L_{Aeq,1h}$) (Top 2)

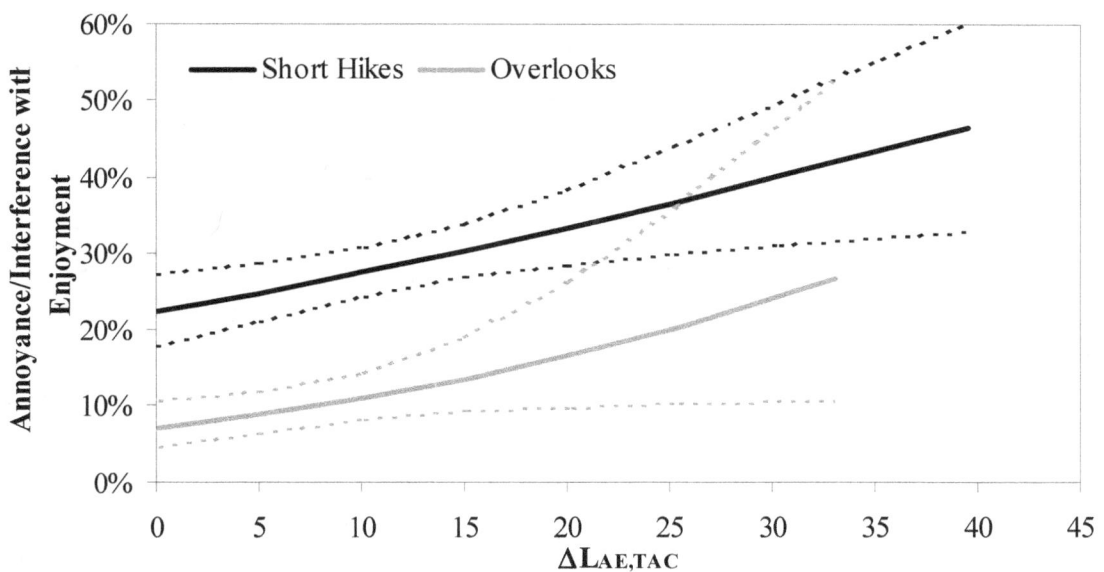

Figure D-11. Annoyance Dose-Response Curves, Change in Sound Exposure Due to Aircraft ($\Delta L_{AE,Tac}$) (Top 3)

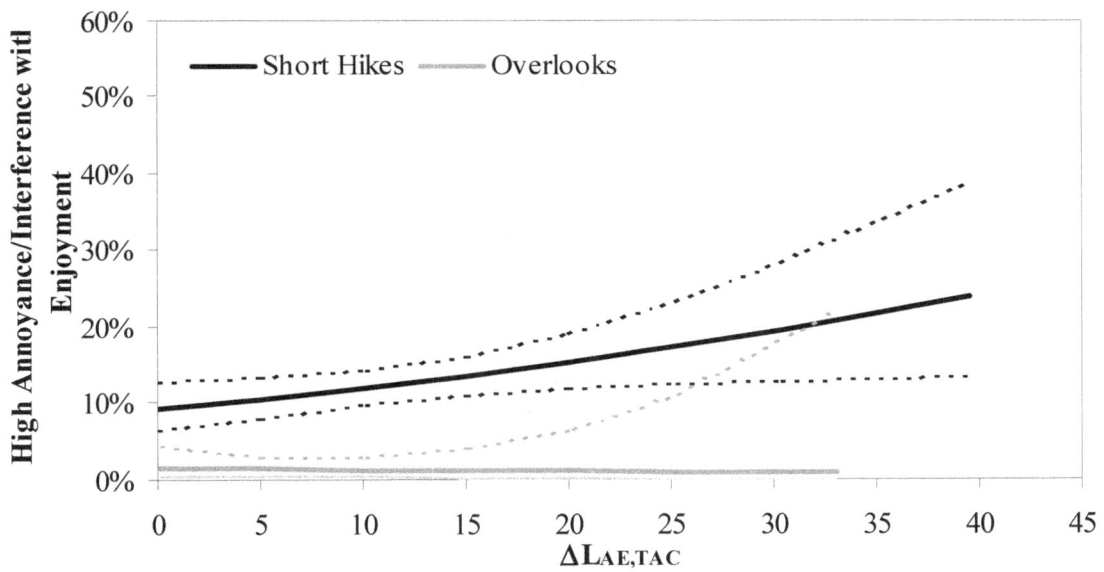

Figure D-12. High Annoyance Dose-Response Curves, Change in Sound Exposure Due to Aircraft ($\Delta L_{AE,Tac}$) (Top 2)

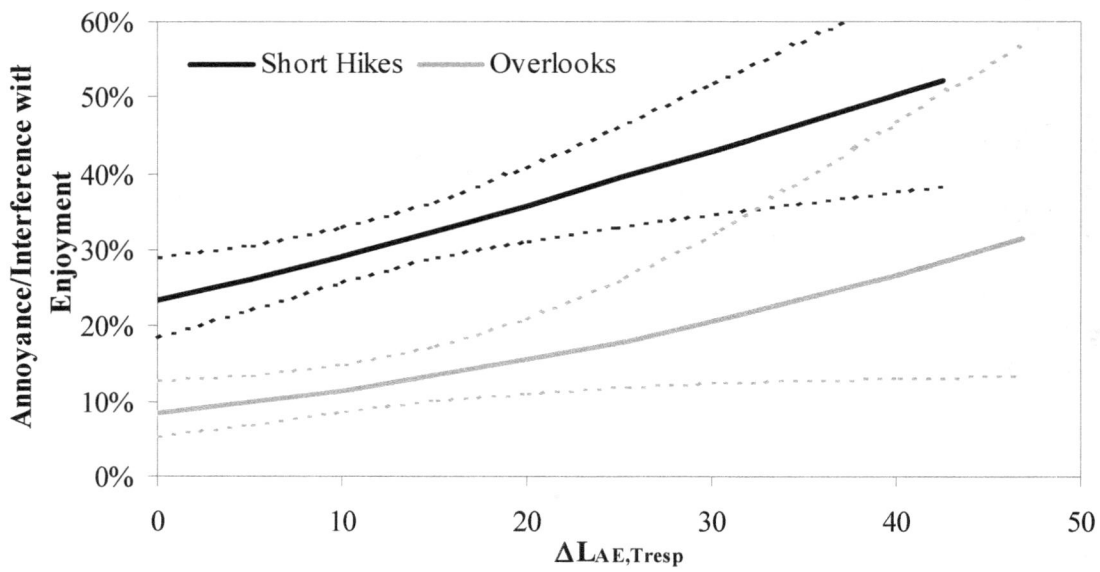

Figure D-13. Annoyance Dose-Response Curves, Change in Sound Exposure Due to Aircraft Normalized to the Respondents Duration ($\Delta L_{AE,Tresp}$) (Top 3)

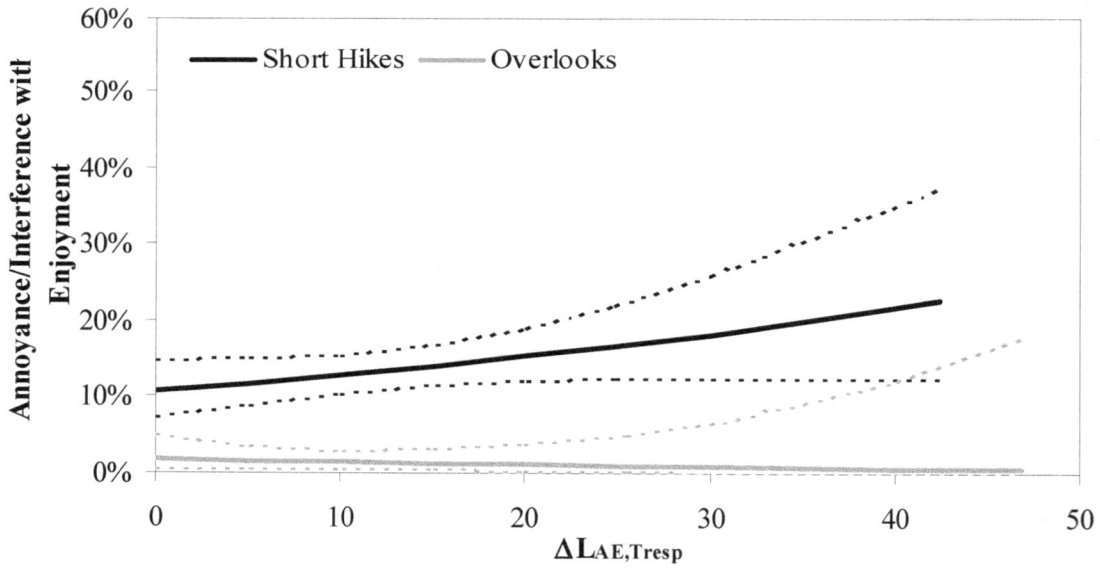

Figure D-14. High Annoyance Dose-Response Curves, Change in Sound Exposure Due to Aircraft Normalized to the Respondents Duration ($\Delta L_{AE,Tresp}$) (Top 2)

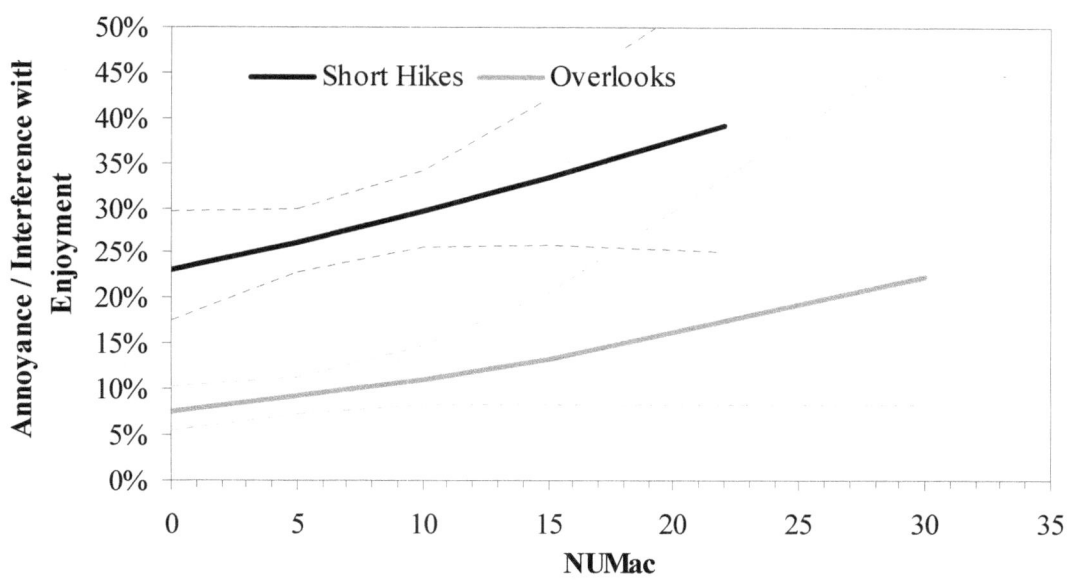

Figure D-15. Dose-Response Curves, Number of Aircraft (NUMac) (Top 3)

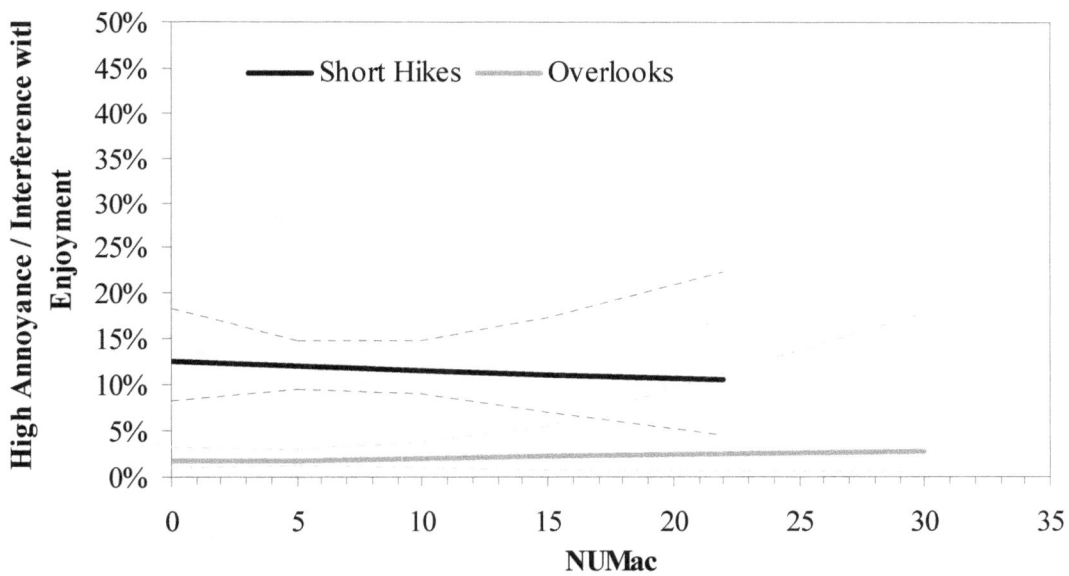

Figure D-16. Dose-Response Curves, Number of Aircraft (NUMac) (Top 2)

Appendix E:
Initial Logistic Regression Analysis

E.1 Logistic Regression Analysis

Tables E-1 and E-2 present the results of the logistic regression analyses performed for each acoustic descriptor for short hikes and overlooks, respectively. Presented are the coefficients of the acoustic descriptor (b_1), whether or not the coefficients are significant (and at what significance level), the constants of the regression (b_0), the Pearson Chi^2 statistics divided by degrees of freedom (dof), and the %Concordance. The significance level represents the level of confidence that the determination of the coefficient is correct, (e.g., if b_1 is determined to be significant at a level of .05, then one can be 95 percent certain the coefficient is significant). The Pearson Chi^2/dof is a criteria used to judge the "goodness of fit" of the model, taking into account the effect of different sample sizes and different numbers of variables. In general, the lower the Pearson Chi^2/dof, the better the model fit. Therefore, it provides a measure of relative "goodness" of models developed for individual noise descriptors. The %Concordance is a statistic used to judge the ability of the model to agree, at least directionally, with the data points. It is calculated by matching all possible pairs of events and non-events (annoyed and not annoyed responses), and calculating the percent of time the model predicts a higher likelihood for occurrence for the event than for the non-event.

Table E-1 Initial Logistic Regression Results, Overlooks

Acoustic Descriptor	Coefficient (b_1)	Coefficient Significant?	Constant (b_0)	Pearson Chi^2/dof	%Concordance
NUM	0.049	Yes*	-2.449	0.993	52.8
$NUM_{ac/hr}$	-0.00	No	-2.201	1.002	00.0
%TA	2.624	Yes***	-6.912	1.038	63.6
%TN	0.301	No	-2.211	1.006	55.1
TAA	1.115	Yes***	-2.764	1.087	67.7
%TAA	1.065	Yes***	-3.687	1.037	65.1
$L_{Aeq,Tac}$	0.010	No	-2.525	1.001	52.1
$L_{Aeq,Tresp}$	0.027	Yes*	-3.107	0.990	61.2
$L_{Aeq,1h}$	0.032	Yes**	-3.072	0.976	63.0
$\Delta L_{AE,Tac}$	0.039	No	-2.419	0.994	58.7
$\Delta L_{AE,Tresp}$	0.029	Yes*	-2.255	0.997	59.0
L_{ASmx}	0.006	No	-2.544	1.001	35.0

*Significant at .05 (95% Certainty) **Significant at .01 (99% Certainty) ***Significant at .001 (99.9% Certainty)

Table E-2. Initial Logistic Regression Results, Short Hikes

Acoustic Descriptor	Coefficient (b_1)	Coefficient Significant?	Constant (b_0)	Pearson Chi^2/dof	%Concordance
NUM_{ac}	0.038	No	-1.142	1.0020	48.8
$NUM_{ac/hr}$	0.006	No	-0.995	1.0019	49.3
%TA	0.874	Yes**	-2.356	1.0074	56.0
%TN	0.368	Yes**	-1.162	1.0020	54.7
TAA	0.4842	Yes*	-1.297	1.0017	53.9
%TAA	0.746	Yes**	-1.985	1.0032	56.1
$L_{Aeq.Tac}$	0.001	No	-0.964	1.0018	18.7
$L_{Aeq.Tresp}$	0.005	No	-1.137	1.0017	47.2
$L_{Aeq.lh}$	0.005	No	-1.109	1.0017	47.3
ΔL	0.023	Yes*	-1.128	1.0013	54.5
$\Delta L_{AE.Tresp}$	0.027	Yes**	-1.110	1.0014	55.9
L_{ASmx}	0.003	No	-1.099	1.0018	44.2

*Significant at .05 (95% Certainty)   **Significant at .01 (99% Certainty)   ***Significant at .001 (99.9% Certainty)

E.2 Model Reliability

Tables E-3 and E-4 show the significance of the acoustic measures for the original data set and for the four bootstrapped data sets for overlooks and short hikes. When a measure was significant at the .05 level, it received a "yes" in the appropriate column. Because it was also useful to know when a measure is "powerful" as well as just significant, an additional column indicates if the measure is significant at the .001 level.

Table E-3. Stability Test Using Bootstrapping, Overlooks

Acoustic Descriptor	Original Data Set Significant? .05	.001	Data Set #1 .05	.001	Data Set #2 Significant? .05	.001	Data Set #3 Significant? .05	.001	Data Set #4 Significant? .05	.001
NUM_{ac}	√		√	√	√		√			
$NUM_{ac/hr}$			√							
%TA	√	√	√	√	√	√	√		√	√
%TN					√					
TAA	√	√	√	√	√	√	√	√	√	√
%TAA	√	√	√	√	√	√	√	√	√	√
$L_{Aeq.Tac}$										
$L_{Aeq.Tresp}$	√				√		√			
$L_{Aeq.lh}$	√		√		√		√		√	
$\Delta L_{AE.Tac}$									√	
$\Delta L_{AE.Tresp}$	√		√							
L_{ASmx}										

Table E-4 Stability Test Using Bootstrapping, Short Hikes

Acoustic Descriptor	Original Data Set Significant?		Data Set #1 Significant?		Data Set #2 Significant?		Data Set #3 Significant?		Data Set #4 Significant?	
	.05	.001	.05	.001	.05	.001	.05	.001	.05	.001
NUM$_{ac}$			√	√			√		√	
NUM$_{ac/hr}$										
%TA	√		√		√		√	√		
%TN	√		√		√	√				
TAA	√		√	√			√	√	√	
%TAA	√		√	√	√		√	√		
L$_{Aeq,Tac}$									√	
L$_{Aeq,Tresp}$									√	
L$_{Aeq,1h}$									√	
ΔL$_{AE,Tac}$	√		√				√		√	
ΔL$_{AE,Tresp}$	√		√				√	√	√	√
L$_{ASmx}$									√	

When combining the results presented in these tables with the results presented for the original data set, it is possible for any given descriptor to receive between 0 and 10 "checks" as a measure of overall reliability. If the descriptor scored a total of zero checks, it would indicate that the descriptor was never significant at the .05 level for any of the data sets. In the same way, a score of 10 checks would indicate that the descriptor was always significant at the .001 level or better. The reliability scores are shown in Table E-5 for overlooks and short hikes.

Table E-5. Reliability Scores for Acoustic Descriptors

Acoustic Descriptor	Reliability Score	
	Overlooks	Short Hikes
NUM$_{ac}$	5	4
NUM$_{ac/hr}$	1	0
%TA	9	5
%TN	1	4
TAA	10	6
%TAA	10	6
L$_{Aeq,Tac}$	0	1
L$_{Aeq,Tresp}$	3	1
L$_{Aeq,1h}$	5	1
ΔL$_{AE,Tac}$	1	4
ΔL$_{AE,Tresp}$	2	6
L$_{ASmx}$	0	1

Only six acoustic descriptors garnered scores equal to or better than a value of five for either overlooks or short hikes: NUM$_{ac}$, %TA, TAA, %TAA, L$_{Aeq,1h}$, and ΔL$_{AE,Tresp}$.

E.3 Performance of Acoustic Descriptors

A component of the exploratory analysis was to determine through statistical analyses, which noise descriptor(s) correlate best with the visitor response data. Table E-6 summarizes the overall descriptor evaluation summarizing the Pearson Chi^2, %C, and

Environmental Measurement and Modeling Division
Volpe Center Acoustics Facility
Study of Visitor Response to Air Tour and Other Aircraft Noise in National Parks

January 2005

reliability. XX indicates that the descriptor is the best choice for that statistical criterion, while X indicates that the descriptor is either the second or third best choice for that criterion. Only eight out of the twelve acoustic descriptors rated first, second or third in at least one performance category: NUMac, %TA, TAA, %TAA, $L_{Aeq,Tresp}$, $L_{Aeq,1h}$, $\Delta L_{AE,Tac}$, and $\Delta L_{AE,Tresp}$.

Table E-6 Overall Performance of Acoustic Descriptors

Acoustic Descriptor	Overlooks			Short Hikes		
	Pearson Chi²/dof	%C	Reliability	Pearson Chi²/dof	%C	Reliability
NUM$_{ac}$	X					
NUM$_{ac/hr}$						
%TA		X	X		X	X
%TN						
TAA		XX	XX	X		XX
%TAA		X	XX		XX	XX
L$_{Aeq,Tac}$						
L$_{Aeq,Tresp}$	X			X		
L$_{Aeq,1h}$	XX		X	X		
ΔL				XX		
ΔL$_{AE,Tresp}$				X	X	XX
L$_{Asmx}$						

Appendix F:
Final Logistic Regression Analysis

F.1 Logistic Regression Analysis

Table F-1 and F-2 present the results of the logistic regression analyses performed for each acoustic descriptor for short hikes and overlooks, respectively. Presented are the coefficient of the acoustic descriptor (b_1), the coefficient of the covariate, whether or not that coefficient is significant (if it was significant, and at what significance level), the constant of the regression (b_0), the coefficient of the first visit covariate (b_2), the Pearson Chi^2 divided by the number of degrees of freedom (dof), and the %Concordance. The significance level represents the level of confidence that the determination of significance is correct, (e.g., if b_1 is determined to be significant at a level of .05, then one can be 95 percent certain the coefficient is significant). The Pearson Chi^2 is a criteria used to judge the "goodness of fit" of the model, taking into account the effect of different sample sizes and different numbers of variables. In general, the lower the statistic, the better the model fit. Therefore, it provides a measure of relative "goodness" of models developed for individual noise descriptors. The %Concordance is a statistic used to judge the ability of the model to agree, at least directionally, with the data points. It is calculated by matching all possible pairs of events and non-events (annoyed and not annoyed responses), and calculating the percent of time the model predicts a higher likelihood for occurrence for the event than for the non-event.

Table F-1 Final Logistic Regression Results, Overlooks

Acoustic Descriptor	Coefficient (b_1)	Coefficient Significant?	Constant (b_0)	Coefficient (b_2)	Pearson Chi^2/dof	%Concordance
NUMac	0.042	No	-3.154	0.653	0.990	58.5
%TA	2.761	Yes***	-8.081	0.799	1.056	64.9
TAA	1.135	Yes***	-3.290	0.461	1.100	68.5
%TAA	1.115	Yes***	-4.353	0.529	1.049	66.2
$L_{Aeq.Tresp}$	0.032	Yes**	-4.384	0.970	0.996	64.6
$L_{Aeq.1h}$	0.037	Yes**	-4.383	1.018	0.971	67.0
$\Delta L_{AE.Tac}$	0.047	Yes*	-3.233	0.667	0.992	61.2
$\Delta L_{AE.Tresp}$	0.034	Yes*	-3.079	0.695	0.994	61.7

*Significant at .05 (95% Certainty) **Significant at .01 (99% Certainty) ***Significant at .001 (99.9% Certainty)

Table F-2 Final Logistic Regression Results, Short Hikes

Acoustic Descriptor	Coefficient (b_1)	Coefficient Significant?	Constant (b_0)	Coefficient (b_2)	Pearson Chi^2/dof	%Concordance
NUMac	0.348	No	-1.863	0.655	1.003	47.3
%TA	1.175	Yes**	-3.318	0.408	1.010	57.5
TAA	0.628	Yes**	-2.099	0.607	1.004	57.6
%TAA	0.887	Yes***	-2.645	0.409	1.004	58.1
$L_{Aeq.Tresp}$	0.009	No	-1.729	0.421	1.001	54.7
$L_{Aeq.1h}$	0.006	No	-1.592	0.418	1.002	53.5
$\Delta L_{AE.Tac}$	0.028	Yes**	-1.779	0.535	1.001	58.4
$\Delta L_{AE.Tresp}$	0.031	Yes**	-1.676	0.473	1.002	58.9

*Significant at .05 (95% Certainty) **Significant at .01 (99% Certainty) ***Significant at .001 (99.9% Certainty)

F.2 Model Reliability

Table F-3 and F-4 show the significance of the acoustic measures for the original data set and for the four bootstrapped data sets for overlooks and short hikes. When a measure was significant at the .05 level, it received a "yes" in the appropriate column. Because it was also useful to know when a measure is "powerful" as well as just significant, an additional column indicates if the measure is significant at the .001 level.

Table F-3 Stability Test Using Bootstrapping, Overlooks

Descriptor	Original Data Set Significant? .05	.001	Data Set #1 Significant? .05	.001	Data Set #2 Significant? .05	.001	Data Set #3 Significant? .05	.001	Data Set #4 Significant? .05	.001
			√	√			√			
%TA	√	√	√	√	√	√	√	√	√	√
TAA	√	√	√	√	√	√	√	√	√	√
%TAA	√	√	√	√	√	√	√		√	√
$L_{Aeq,Tresp}$	√				√		√		√	
$L_{Aeq,1h}$	√		√				√		√	√
$\Delta L_{AE,Tac}$	√				√				√	
$\Delta L_{AE,Tresp}$	√		√		√					

Table F-4 Stability Test Using Bootstrapping, Short Hikes

Acoustic Descriptor	Original Data Set Significant? .05	.001	Data Set #1 Significant? .05	.001	Data Set #2 Significant? .05	.001	Data Set #3 Significant? .05	.001	Data Set #4 Significant? .05	.001
NUMac			√							
%TA	√		√		√	√	√	√		
TAA	√		√	√			√			
%TAA	√	√	√	√	√	√	√	√		
$L_{Aeq,Tresp}$			√						√	
$L_{Aeq,1h}$			√						√	
$\Delta L_{AE,Tac}$	√		√	√			√	√	√	√
$\Delta L_{AE,Tresp}$	√		√	√	√	√	√	√	√	√

When combining the results presented in these tables with the results presented for the original data set, it is possible for any given descriptor to receive between 0 and 10 "checks" as a measure of overall reliability. If the descriptor scored a total of zero checks, it would indicate that the descriptor was never significant at the .05 level for any of the data sets. In the same way, a score of 10 checks would indicate that the descriptor was always significant at the .001 level or better. The reliability scores are shown in Table F-5 for overlooks and short hikes.

Table F-5 Reliability Scores for Acoustic Descriptors

Acoustic Descriptor	Reliability Score	
	Overlooks	Short Hikes
NUMac	3	1
%TA	10	6
TAA	10	5
%TAA	9	8
$L_{Aeq,Tresp}$	4	2
$L_{Aeq,1h}$	6	2
$\Delta L_{AE,Tac}$	3	7
$\Delta L_{AE,Tresp}$	3	8

F.3 Final Performance of Acoustic Descriptors

A component of the exploratory analysis was to determine through statistical analyses, which noise descriptor(s) correlate best with the visitor response data. Table F-6 summarizes the overall descriptor evaluation summarizing the Pearson Chi^2, %C, and reliability. XX indicates that the descriptor is the best choice for that statistical criterion, while X indicates that the descriptor is either the second or the third best choice for that criterion.

Table F-6 Final Performance of Acoustic Descriptors

Acoustic Descriptor	Overlooks			Short Hikes		
	Pearson Chi^2/dof	%C	Reliability	Pearson Chi^2/dof	%C	Reliability
NUMac	X			X		
%TA			XX			X
TAA		XX	XX			
%TAA		X	X		X	XX
$L_{Aeq,Tresp}$				XX		
$L_{Aeq,1h}$	XX	X	X	X		
$\Delta L_{AE,Tac}$	X			XX	X	X
$\Delta L_{AE,Tresp}$				X	XX	XX

The descriptors that showed the best overall performance were %TAA, $L_{Aeq,1h}$, $\Delta L_{AE,Tac}$, and $\Delta L_{AE,Tresp}$. When the site types are considered separately, the descriptors that showed the best performance for overlooks were %TAA and $L_{Aeq,1h}$. For short hikes, the best descriptors were $\Delta L_{AE,Tac}$ and $\Delta L_{AE,Tresp}$. Graphical presentations of the final dose-response regressions are displayed in Appendix D for all eight acoustic descriptors, utilizing both the top three and top two dichotomization.

Appendix G:
Study Limitations

The dose-response curves presented in Section 3 and in Appendix D may have certain underlying biases that deserve consideration. Although these biases are important to consider, one must remember that this study represents best available data short of additional field research. Section G.1 discusses any underlying site bias that may influence the curves, while Section G.2 discusses the certainty of the dose-response curves at the upper and lower bounds.

G.1 Site Bias

Figures G-1 through G-8 and Tables G-1 through G-8 show the relative distribution of data by site for overlooks as a function of each acoustic descriptor, summarized as follows:

- The data from Point Imperial may influence the upper end of the dose-response curve for %TAA and TAA.
- The data from both Point Imperial and Pima Point may influence the upper end of the dose response curves for $L_{Aeq,Tresp}$, $L_{Aeq,1h}$, and $\Delta L_{AE,Tac}$.

Figures G-9 through G-16 and Tables G-9 through G-16 show the relative distribution of data by site for short hikes as a function of each acoustic descriptor, summarized as follows:

- The data from BCNP may unduly influence the upper end of the dose-response curve for %TA, %TAA, and NUMac.
- The data at Hawaii Volcanoes may influence the upper end of the dose-response curve for $L_{Aeq,Tresp}$ and $L_{Aeq,1h.}$
- The data for the dose-response curves for $\Delta L_{AE,Tac}$ falls into three bands; BCNP at the lower end of the range, Haleakala in the mid-range, and Hawaii Volcanoes at the upper end of the range.

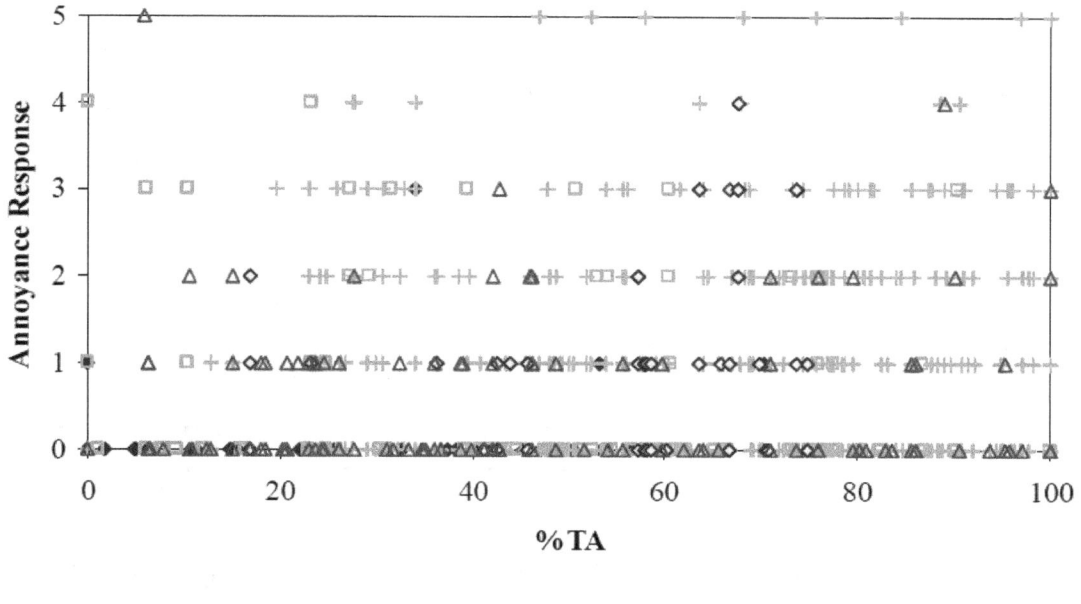

Figure G-1. Distribution of Responses by Site and %TA - Overlooks

Table G-1. Percentage of Respondents by Site and %TA - Overlooks

TA (%)	Rainbow Point	Fairyland	Point Imperial	Bryce Point	Pima Point	Lipan Point
All Data	4.9	12.8	43.0	4.6	17.3	17.5
0-10	21.2	33.3	3.0	0.0	0.0	42.4
10-20	14.9	21.3	10.6	6.4	0.0	46.8
20-30	7.2	13.0	47.8	1.4	0.0	30.4
30-40	5.5	9.6	41.1	1.4	4.1	38.4
40-50	6.1	14.3	56.1	6.1	2.0	15.3
50-60	12.9	18.8	44.7	14.1	2.4	7.1
60-70	1.9	15.5	48.5	11.7	13.6	8.7
70-80	2.9	12.5	52.2	5.9	16.2	10.3
80-90	0.0	3.9	38.3	0.0	44.5	13.3
90-100	0.0	9.0	42.8	0.0	37.3	10.8

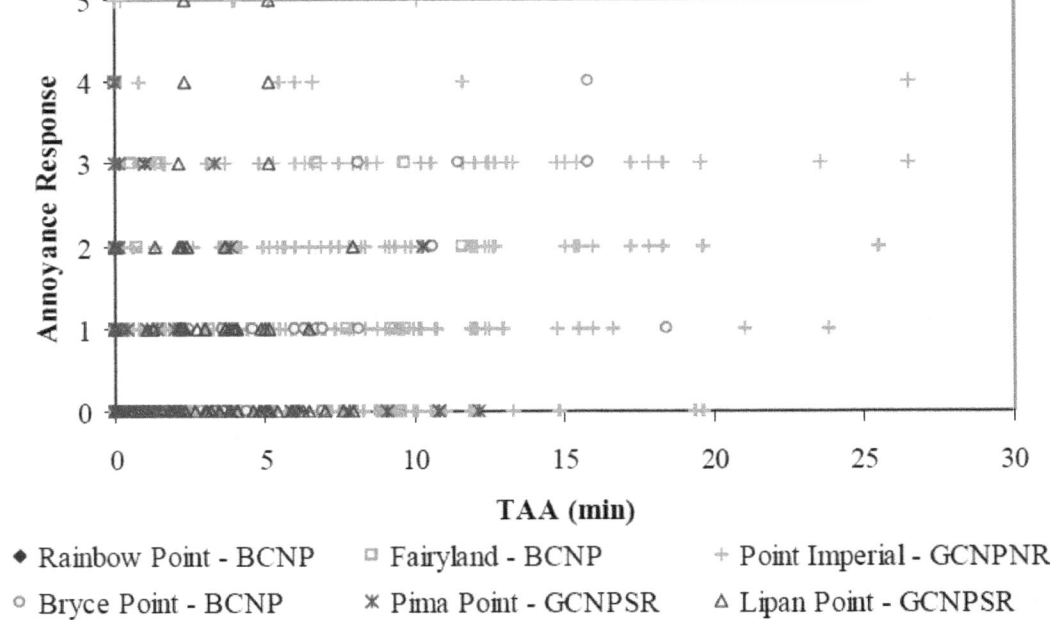

Figure G-2. **Distribution of Responses by Site and TAA - Overlooks**

Table G-2. Percentage of Respondents by Site and TAA - Overlooks

TAA	Rainbow Point	Fairyland	Point Imperial	Bryce Point	Pima Point	Lipan Point
All Data	0.0	12.2	43.2	4.6	17.4	17.6
0-5	7.5	15.1	29.0	2.9	24.6	0.0
5-10	0.0	8.9	63.9	7.9	2.5	0.0
10-15	0.0	4.2	83.3	5.6	6.9	0.0
15-20	0.0	0.0	81.3	15.6	0.0	0.0
>20	0.0	0.0	100.0	0.0	0.0	0.0

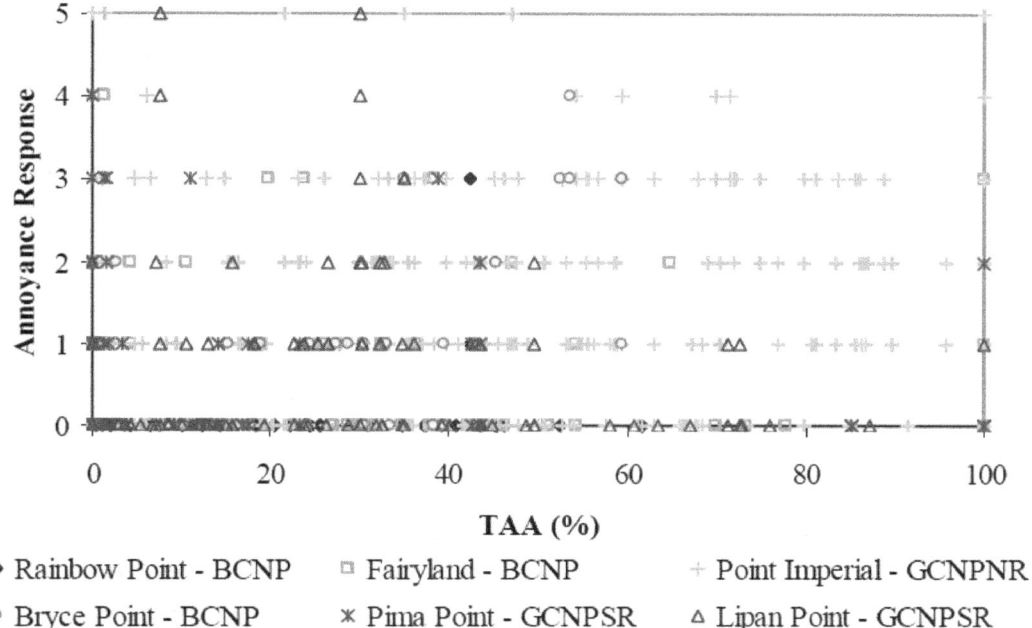

Figure G-3. Distribution of Responses by Site and %TAA - Overlooks

Table G-3. Percentage of Respondents by Site and %TAA - Overlooks

TAA (%)	Rainbow Point	Fairyland	Point Imperial	Bryce Point	Pima Point	Lipan Point
All Data	4.9	12.8	43.0	4.6	17.3	17.5
0-10	5.0	14.0	21.7	1.3	43.5	14.4
10-20	4.8	13.6	41.6	8.0	10.4	21.6
20-30	8.2	13.3	46.9	5.1	2.0	24.5
30-40	5.5	14.5	42.7	12.7	0.9	23.6
40-50	9.0	12.4	50.6	3.4	6.7	18.0
50-60	1.9	7.4	74.1	13.0	0.0	3.7
60-70	5.6	5.6	69.4	0.0	0.0	19.4
70-80	0.0	9.1	60.6	0.0	0.0	30.3
80-90	0.0	0.0	83.3	0.0	6.7	10.0
90-100	0.0	10.5	64.9	0.0	14.0	10.5

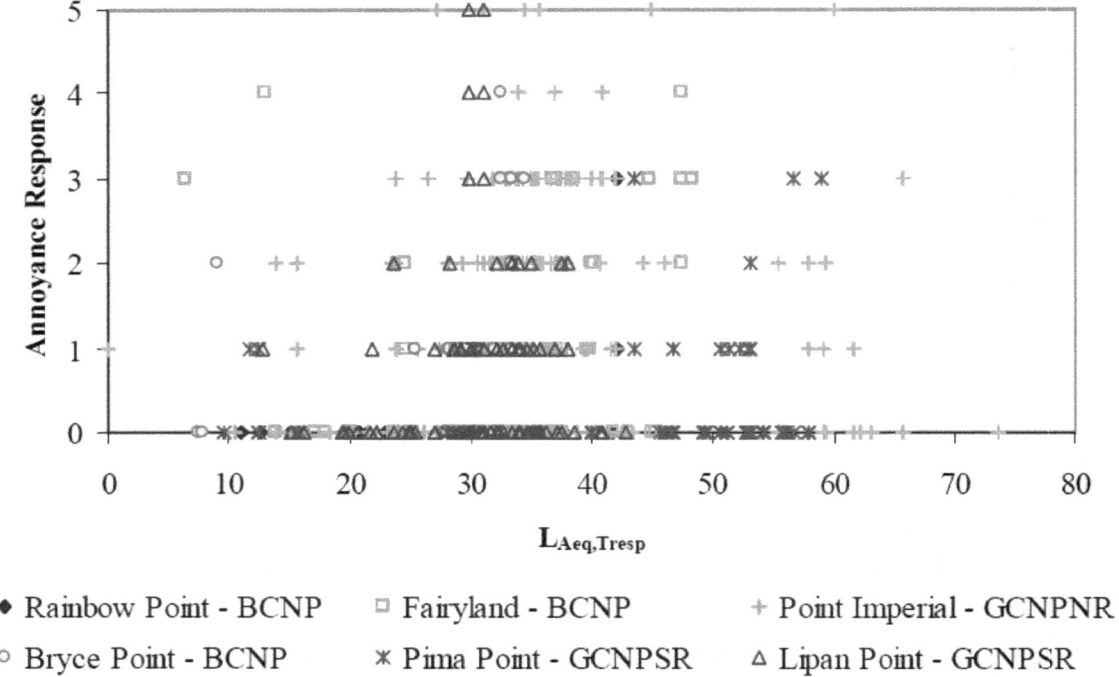

Figure G-4. Distribution of Responses by Site and $L_{Aeq,Tresp}$ - Overlooks

Table G-4. Percentage of Respondents by Site and $L_{Aeq,Tresp}$ - Overlooks

$L_{Aeq,Tresp}$	Rainbow Point	Fairyland	Point Imperial	Bryce Point	Pima Point	Lipan Point
	5.0	13.0	46.3	6.0	9.8	19.9
0-5	0.0	0.0	100.0	0.0	0.0	0.0
5-10	0.0	12.5	0.0	62.5	25.0	0.0
10-15	13.3	13.3	33.3	0.0	26.7	13.3
15-20	12.1	18.2	21.2	0.0	9.1	39.4
20-25	21.6	16.2	27.0	0.0	0.0	35.1
25-30	4.4	9.6	43.9	14.9	4.4	22.8
30-35	3.3	14.8	48.6	9.5	1.4	22.4
35-40	3.1	13.1	60.0	0.0	3.1	20.6
40-45	9.1	15.9	56.8	0.0	4.5	13.6
45-50	0.0	31.6	10.5	0.0	57.9	0.0
>50	0.0	0.0	43.3	0.0	56.7	0.0

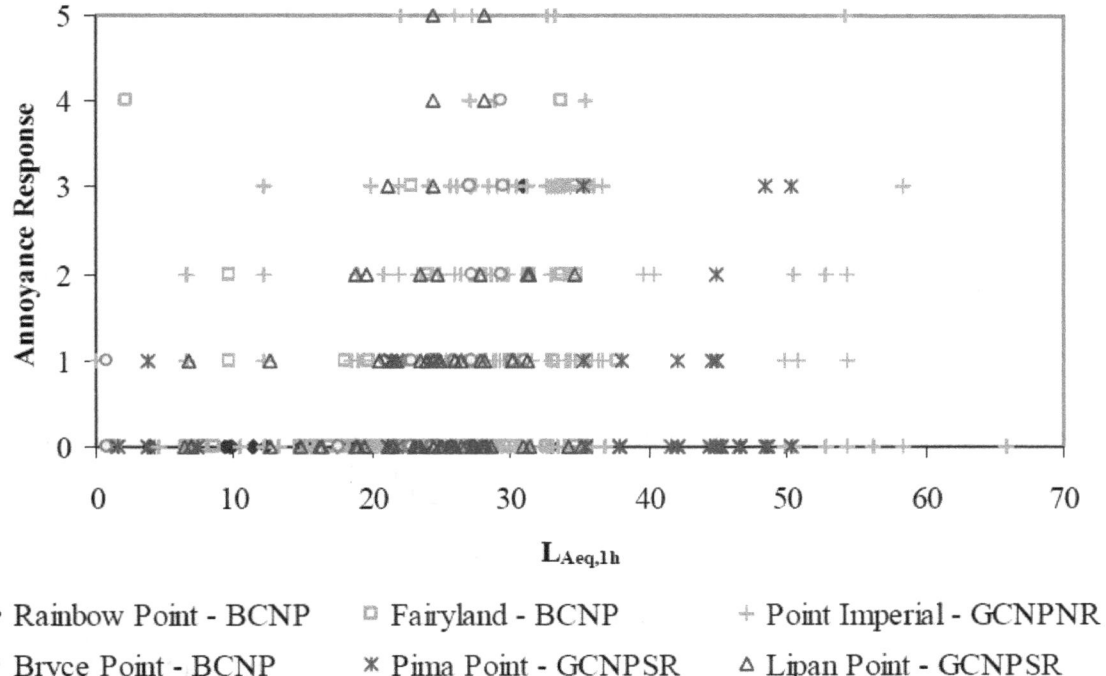

♦ Rainbow Point - BCNP   □ Fairyland - BCNP   + Point Imperial - GCNPNR

○ Bryce Point - BCNP   ✳ Pima Point - GCNPSR   △ Lipan Point - GCNPSR

Figure G-5. Distribution of Responses by Site and $L_{Aeq,1h}$ - Overlooks

Table G-5. Percentage of Respondents by Site and $L_{Aeq,1h}$ - Overlooks

$L_{Aeq,1h}$	Rainbow Point	Fairyland	Point Imperial	Point	Pima Point	Lipan Point
All Data	5.2	13.1	46.0	6.4	8.5	20.9
0-5	14.3	9.5	23.8	23.8	28.6	0.0
5-10	13.8	27.6	24.1	0.0	10.3	24.1
10-15	20.0	3.3	30.0	0.0	0.0	46.7
15-20	12.7	23.8	25.4	1.6	0.0	36.5
20-25	3.5	16.0	34.7	12.5	5.6	27.8
25-30	2.1	10.6	59.8	7.9	1.1	18.5
30-35	3.4	14.7	63.8	2.6	0.0	15.5
35-40	0.0	0.0	9.5	0.0	90.5	0.0
40-45	0.0	0.0	11.8	0.0	88.2	0.0
>45	0.0	0.0	88.9	0.0	11.1	0.0

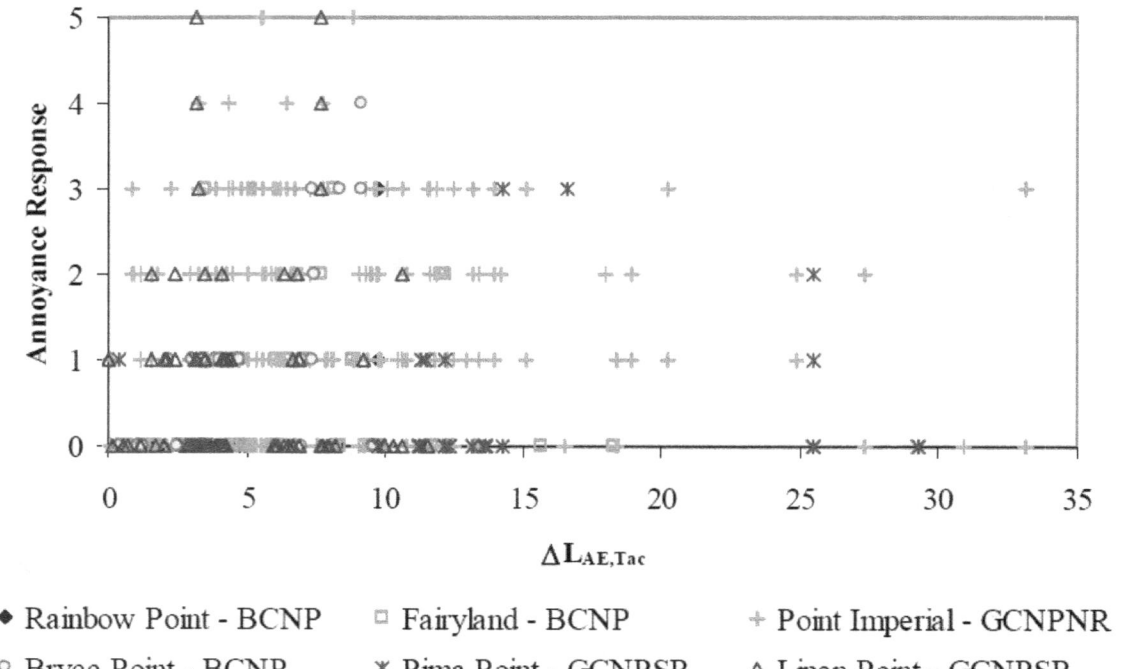

♦ Rainbow Point - BCNP   □ Fairyland - BCNP   + Point Imperial - GCNPNR

○ Bryce Point - BCNP   * Pima Point - GCNPSR   △ Lipan Point - GCNPSR

Figure G-6. Distribution of Responses by Site and $\Delta L_{AE,Tac}$ - Overlooks

Table G-6. Percentage of Respondents by Site and $\Delta L_{AE,Tac}$ - Overlooks

$\Delta L_{AE,Tac}$	Rainbow Point	Fairyland	Point Imperial	Bryce Point	Pima Point	Lipan Point
All Data	5.4	10.6	50.3	6.7	6.7	20.4
0-5	10.9	10.5	37.5	10.1	2.6	28.5
5-10	1.8	12.4	61.0	6.4	0.9	17.4
10-15	0.0	5.3	58.9	0.0	24.2	11.6
15-20	0.0	31.3	62.5	0.0	6.3	0.0
20-25	0.0	0.0	100.0	0.0	0.0	0.0
>25	0.0	0.0	42.9	0.0	57.1	0.0

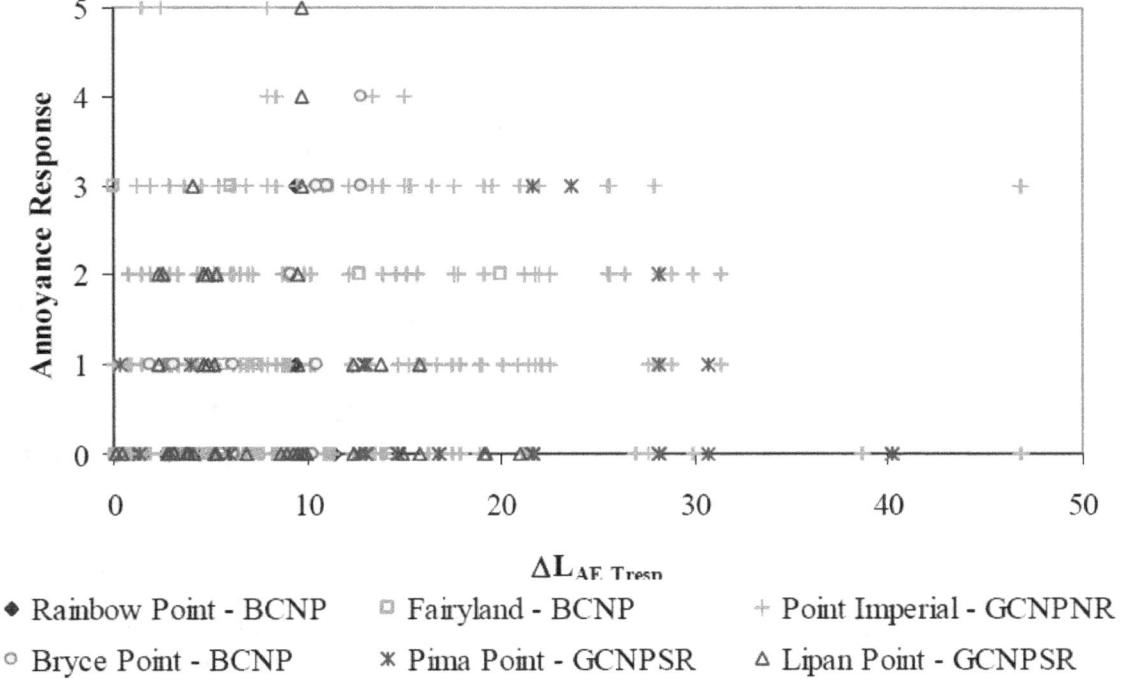

Figure G-7. Distribution of Responses by Site and $\Delta L_{AE,Tresp}$ - Overlooks

Table G-7. Percentage of Respondents by Site and $\Delta L_{AE,Tresp}$ - Overlooks

$\Delta L_{AE,Tresp}$	Rainbow Point	Fairyland	Point Imperial	Bryce Point	Pima Point	Lipan Point
All Data	3.3	11.6	55.0	5.7	7.9	16.5
0-5	7.5	13.2	46.5	8.8	3.1	20.8
5-10	1.4	17.0	53.9	3.5	0.7	23.4
10-15	2.8	12.7	49.3	12.7	15.5	7.0
15-20	0.0	0.0	79.2	0.0	4.2	16.7
20-25	0.0	8.8	55.9	0.0	29.4	5.9
>25	0.0	0.0	73.7	0.0	26.3	0.0

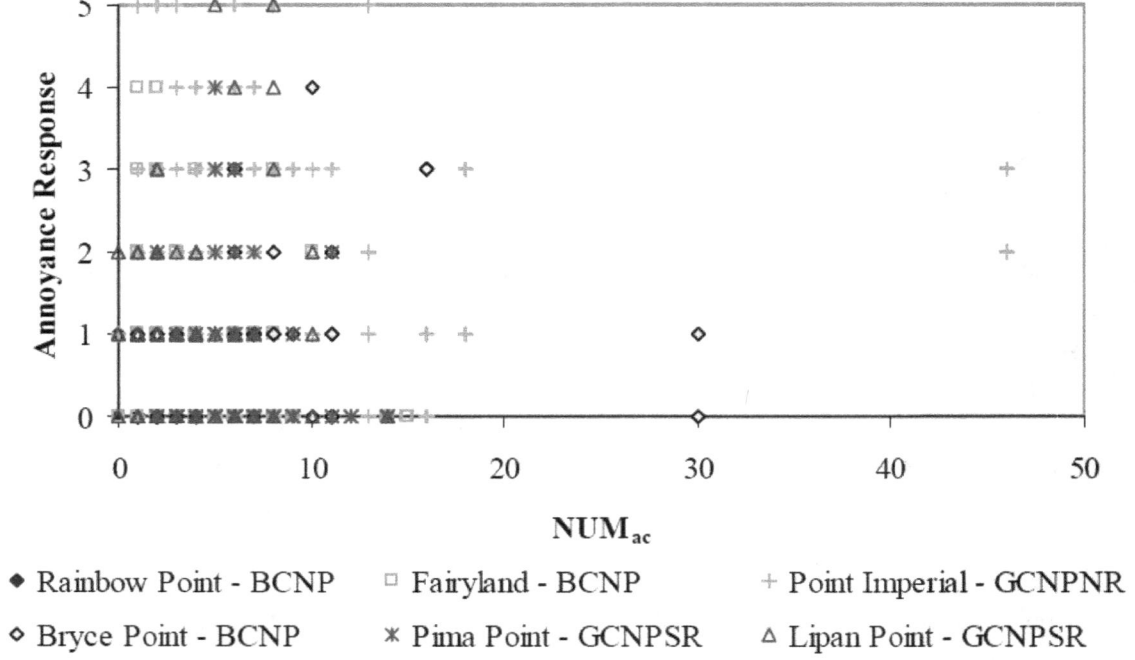

Figure G-8. Distribution of Responses by Site and NUMac - Overlooks

Table G-8. Percentage of Respondents by Site and NUMac - Overlooks

NUMac	Rainbow Point	Fairyland	Point Imperial	Bryce Point	Pima Point	Point
All Data	4.9	12.7	43.2	4.6	17.4	17.2
0-5	7.4	15.5	42.2	1.4	12.2	21.3
6-10	0.0	11.7	88.3	7.7	29.6	10.0
11-15	0.0	31.3	68.8	25.7	25.7	2.9
16-20	0.0	0.0	100.0	42.9	0.0	0.0
>20	0.0	0.0	100.0	50.0	0.0	0.0

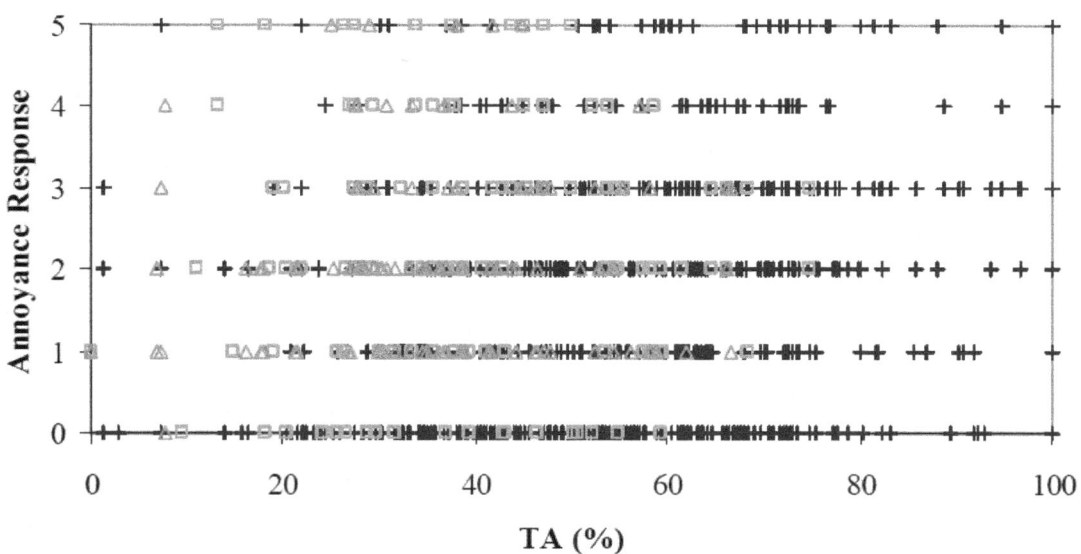

+ Queens Garden, BCNP   □ Sliding Sands, Haleakala

△ Wahaula Temple, Hawaii Volcanoes

Figure G-9. Distribution of Responses by Site and %TA – Short Hikes

Table G-9. Percentage of Respondents by Site and %TA - Short Hikes

TA (%)	BCNP	Sliding Sands	Wahaula Temple
All Data	75.4	13.9	10.7
0-10	52.9	11.8	35.3
10-20	29.6	48.1	22.2
20-30	46.3	33.1	20.7
30-40	59.3	18.7	22.0
40-50	73.7	12.7	13.6
50-60	77.6	15.8	6.6
60-70	92.5	4.3	3.2
70-80	98.3	1.7	0.0
80-90	100.0	0.0	0.0
90-100	100.0	0.0	0.0

Environmental Measurement and Modeling Division
Volpe Center Acoustics Facility
Study of Visitor Response to Air Tour and Other Aircraft Noise in National Parks

January 2005

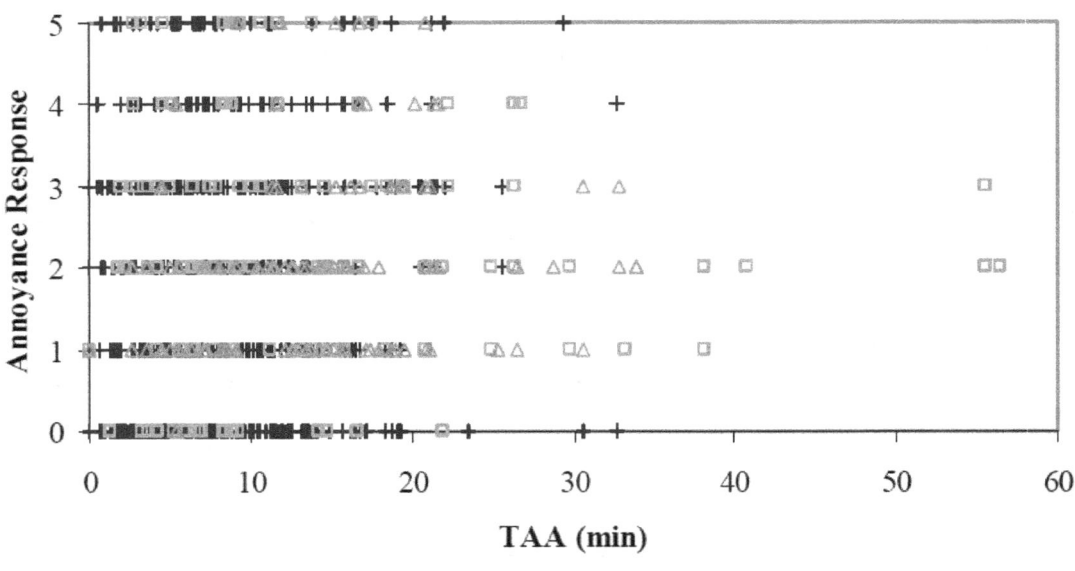

+ Queens Garden, BCNP   □ Sliding Sands, Haleakala
△ Wahaula Temple, Hawaii Volcanoes

Figure G-10. Distribution of Responses by Site and TAA - Short Hikes

Table G-10. Percentage of Respondents by Site and TAA - Short Hikes

TAA	BCNP	Sliding Sands	Wahauala Temple
All Data	75.2	14.0	10.9
0-5	86.0	10.9	3.1
5-10	81.6	13.9	4.5
10-15	72.5	12.4	15.0
15-20	53.8	14.2	32.1
20-25	37.5	20.0	42.5
25-30	17.6	41.2	41.2
30-35	27.3	9.1	63.6
>35	0.0	100.0	0.0

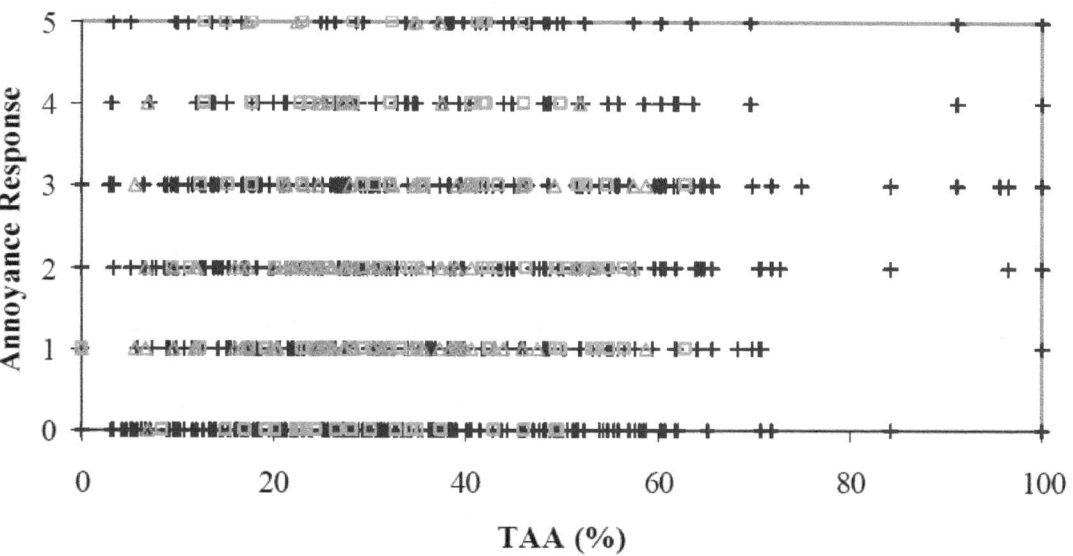

+ Queens Garden, BCNP   □ Sliding Sands, Haleakala
△ Wahaula Temple, Hawaii Volcanoes

Figure G-11. Distribution of Responses by Site and %TAA - Short Hikes

Table G-11. Percentage of Respondents by Site and %TAA - Short Hikes

TAA (%)	BCNP	Haleakala	Hawaii Volcanoes
All Data	75.2	14.0	10.9
0-10	83.3	4.9	11.8
10-20	79.8	12.5	7.7
20-30	67.9	16.2	15.9
30-40	68.7	14.8	16.5
40-50	72.0	21.7	6.3
50-60	76.5	15.1	8.4
60-70	96.0	4.0	0.0
70-80	100.0	0.0	0.0
80-90	100.0	0.0	0.0
90-100	100.0	0.0	0.0

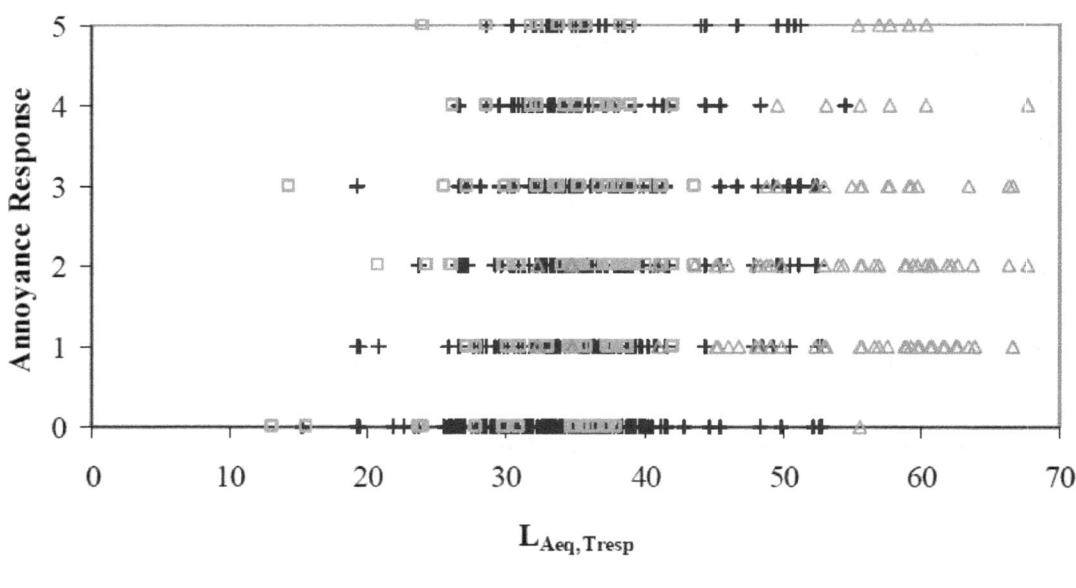

+ Queens Garden, BCNP   □ Sliding Sands, Haleakala

△ Wahaula Temple, Hawaii Volcanoes

Figure G-12. Distribution of Responses by Site and $L_{Aeq,Tresp}$ - Short Hikes

Table G-12. Percentage of Respondents by Site and $L_{Aeq,Tresp}$ - Short Hikes

$L_{Aeq,Tresp}$	BCNP	Haleakala	Hawaii Volcanoes
All Data	77.2	14.8	8.0
<10	0.0	100.0	0.0
10-15	85.7	14.3	0.0
15-20	63.2	36.8	0.0
20-25	86.1	13.9	0.0
25-30	85.8	13.3	0.9
30-35	78.8	21.2	0.0
35-40	80.6	15.3	4.2
40-45	51.1	0.0	48.9
45-50	73.9	0.0	26.1
>50	0.0	0.0	100.0

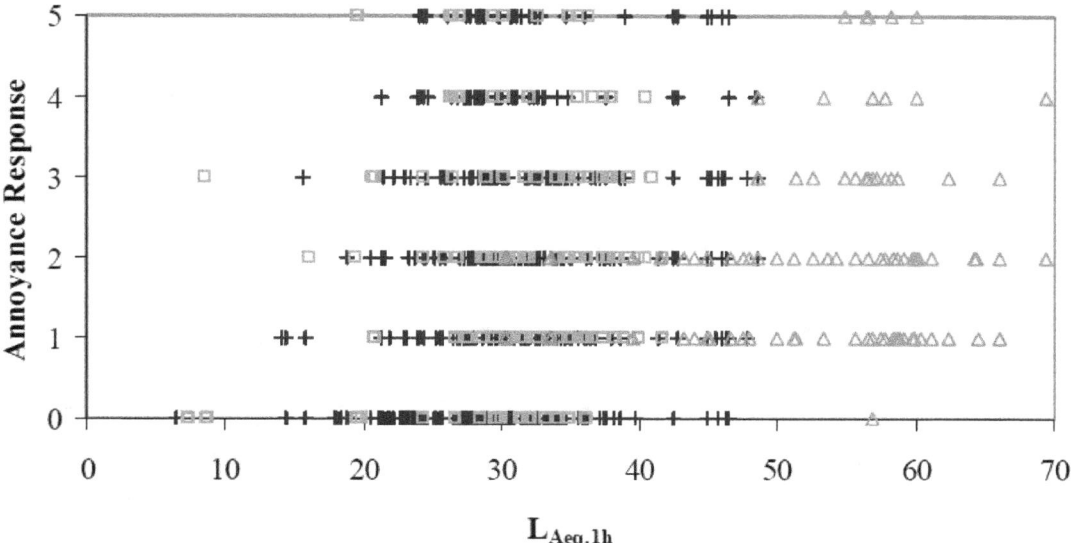

+ Queens Garden - BNCP   □ Sliding Sands - Haleakala

△ Wahaula Temple - Hawaii Volcanoes

Figure G-13. Distribution of Responses by Site and $L_{Aeq,1h}$ - Short Hikes

Table G-13. Percentage of Respondents by Site and $L_{Aeq,1h}$ - Short Hikes

$L_{Aeq,Tresp}$	BCNP	Haleakala	Hawaii Volcanoes
	74.7	14.3	10.9
<10	16.7	83.3	0.0
10-15	100.0	0.0	0.0
15-20	66.7	33.3	0.0
20-25	89.0	11.0	0.0
25-30	88.6	11.4	0.0
30-35	81.9	17.0	1.1
35-40	68.1	30.2	1.7
40-45	56.4	15.4	28.2
45-50	75.9	0.0	24.1
>50	0.0	0.0	100.0

Environmental Measurement and Modeling Division
Volpe Center Acoustics Facility
Study of Visitor Response to Air Tour and Other Aircraft Noise in National Parks

January 2005

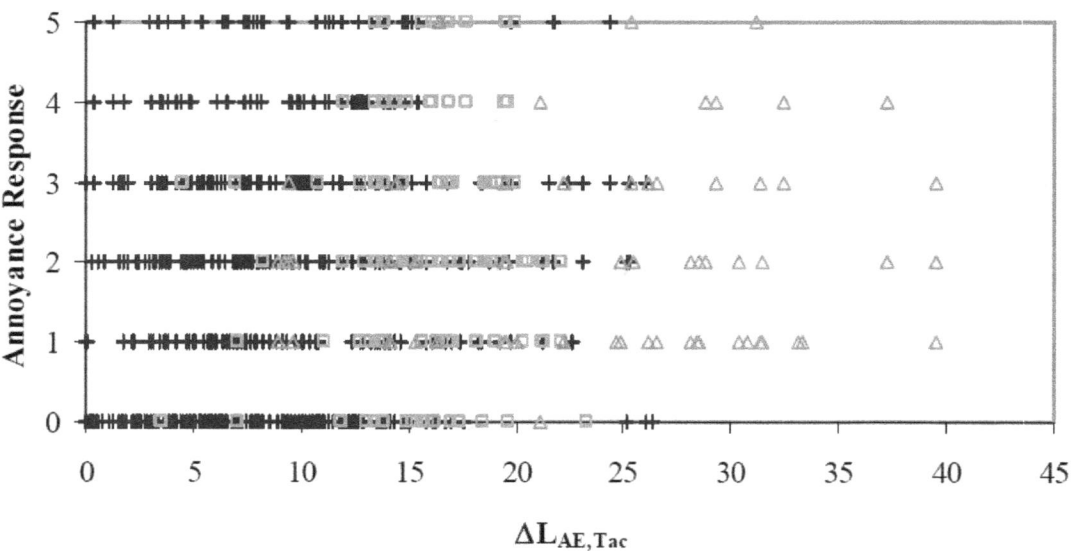

+ Queens Garden, BCNP
□ Sliding Sands, Haleakala
△ Wahaula Temple, Hawaii Volcanoes

Figure G-14. Distribution of Responses by Site and $\Delta L_{AE,Tac}$ - Short Hikes

Table G-14. Percentage of Respondents by Site and $\Delta L_{AE,Tac}$ - Short Hikes

$\Delta L_{AE,Tac}$	BCNP	Haleakala	Hawaii Volcanoes
All Data	75.0	17.0	8.0
0-5	94.5	4.4	1.1
5-10	82.4	15.0	2.6
10-15	75.6	20.2	4.2
15-20	59.4	36.0	4.6
20-25	66.0	15.1	18.9
25-30	43.2	0.0	56.8
>30	39.1	0.0	60.9

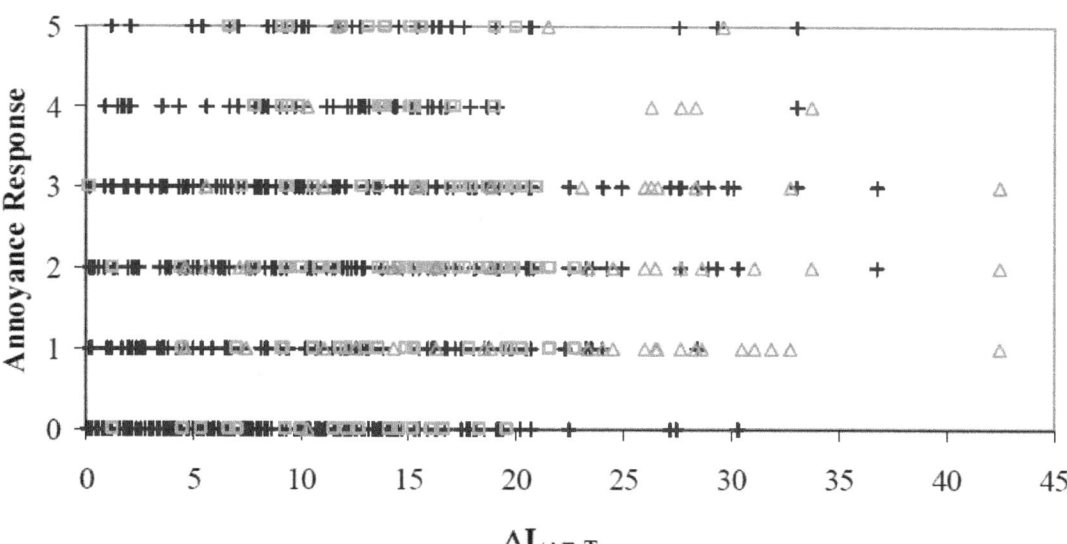

+ Queens Garden, BCNP   □ Sliding Sands, Haleakala

△ Wahaula Temple, Hawaii Volcanoes

Figure G-15. Distribution of Responses by Site and $\Delta L_{AE,Tresp}$ - Short Hikes

Table G-15. Percentage of Respondents by Site and $\Delta L_{AE,Tresp}$ - Short Hikes

$\Delta L_{AE,Tresp}$	BCNP	Haleakala	Hawaii Volcanoes
All Data	77.5	15.2	7.3
0-5	97.8	2.2	0.0
5-10	95.8	1.6	2.6
10-15	79.4	19.6	1.1
15-20	37.1	55.6	7.3
20-25	37.1	34.3	28.6
25-30	27.6	0.0	72.4
>30	0.0	0.0	100.0

Environmental Measurement and Modeling Division
Volpe Center Acoustics Facility
Study of Visitor Response to Air Tour and Other Aircraft Noise in National Parks

January 2005

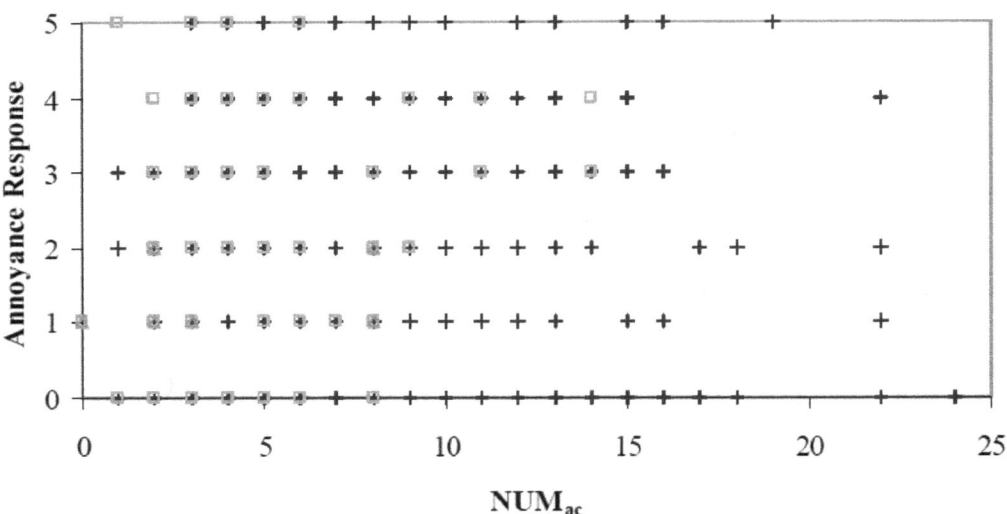

+ Queens Garden, BCNP   □ Sliding Sands, Haleakala
△ Wahaula Temple, Hawaii Volcanoes

Figure G-16. Distribution of Responses by Site and NUMac - Short Hikes

Table G-16. Percentage of Respondents by Site and NUMac - Short Hikes

NUMac	BCNP	Haleakala	Hawaii Volcanoes
All Data	86.6	12.6	0.8
0-5	72.2	26.2	1.7
6-10	93.8	5.7	0.4
11-15	97.0	3.0	0.0
16-20	100.0	0.0	0.0
21-25	100.0	0.0	0.0

G.2 Confidence Intervals at Upper/Lower Tails of the Dose-Response Curves

The confidence intervals of the dose-response curves at the upper and lower tails of the curves were re-examined by plotting the average and 95% confidence intervals of the data in bins along with the regression line and the 95% confidence interval of the regression line. In this manner, the confidence of the data in each region of the regression can be examined separately, and compared to the confidence of the regression curve as a whole.

Figures G-17 through G-24 present graphics for overlooks. These graphics shows that:
- Although the number of data points that exist below 10%TA and %TAA are small, the confidence intervals around the averages are relatively small. This would seem to suggest that there is enough certainty in this data (and also the data over the entire range of these curves).
- There does not seem to be a lot of certainty in the data at the high end of the range for $\Delta L_{AE,Tac}$, $\Delta L_{AE,Tresp}$, and NUMac. In this case, the small number of data points is accompanied by relatively large confidence intervals around the averages.

Figures G-25 through G-32 present graphics for short hikes. These graphics show that:
- There does not seem to be a lot of certainty in the data below 5% TA and TAA. In this case, the low numbers of data points are accompanied by relatively large confidence intervals around the averages. The confidence interval around the lowest average is a result of a two respondents who reported very and extremely annoyed below 3%.
- There is not a lot of certainty in the data above 35 dBA for the $\Delta L_{AE,Tac}$ and $\Delta L_{AE,Tresp}$ descriptors.
- The curves do not follow the data point averages at the lower end of the range for the $L_{Aeq,Tresp}$ and $L_{Aeq,1h}$ descriptors.

These graphics may provide one explanation for a presumed shortcoming of the logistic regression methodology. Namely, that, in many cases, the predicted response will be greater than zero in the absence of an aircraft noise dose. The graphics for %TAA show that the data is very sparse in the low-dose regions, and the predictions are heavily influenced by a few respondents. It is assumed that if an adequate number of data points were available at low doses, these curves would most approach a zero/zero intercept.

Environmental Measurement and Modeling Division
Volpe Center Acoustics Facility
Study of Visitor Response to Air Tour and Other Aircraft Noise in National Parks

January 2005

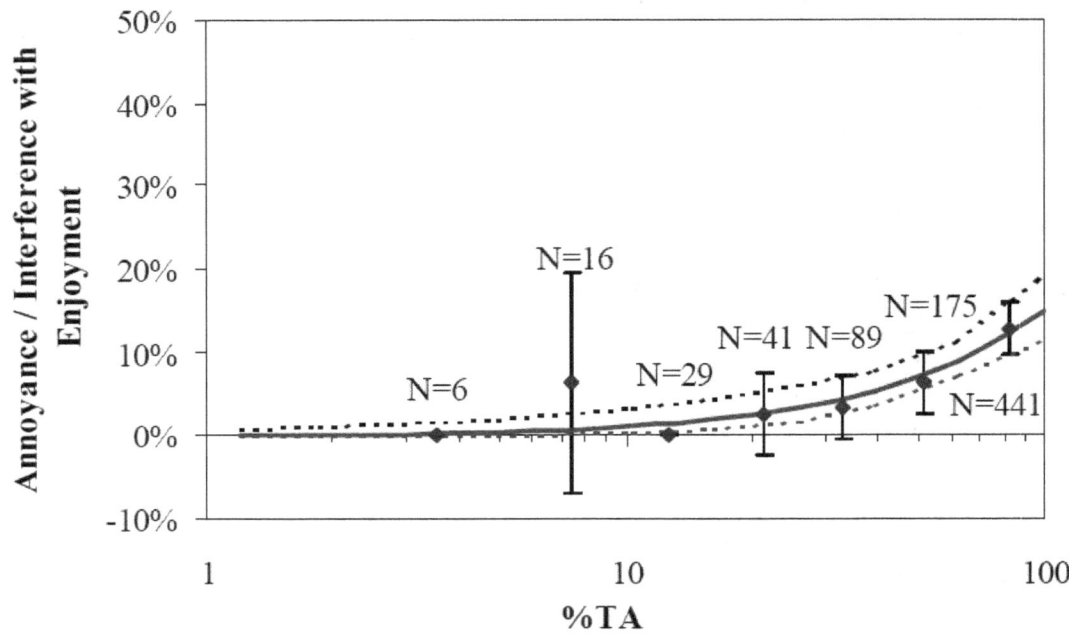

Figure G-17. Grouped Confidence Intervals vs. Regression Confidence Intervals, Overlooks, %TA

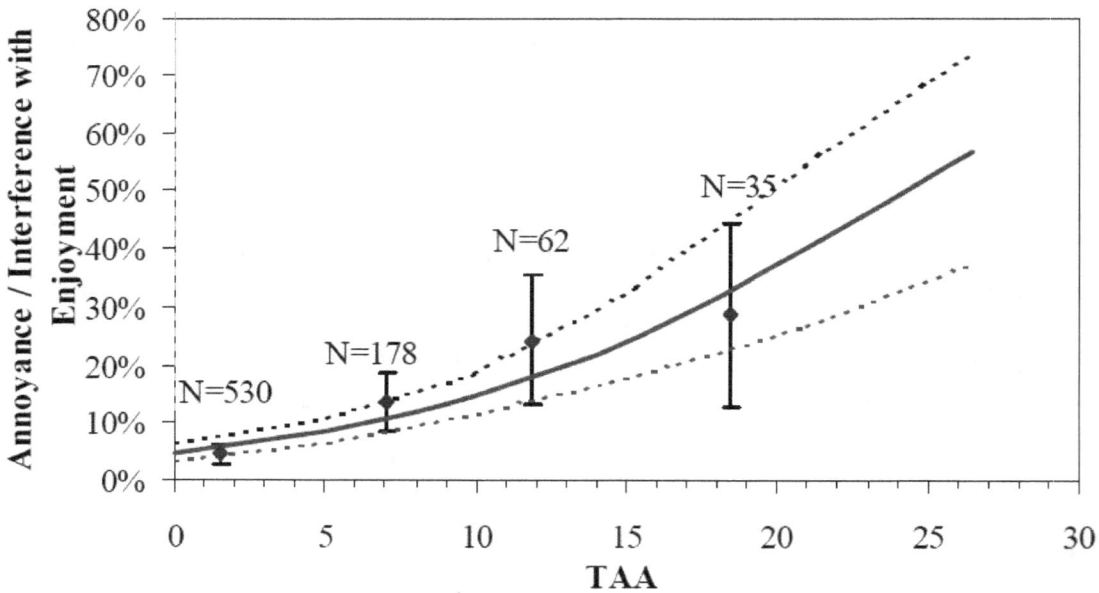

Figure G-18. Grouped Confidence Intervals vs. Regression Confidence Intervals, Overlooks, TAA

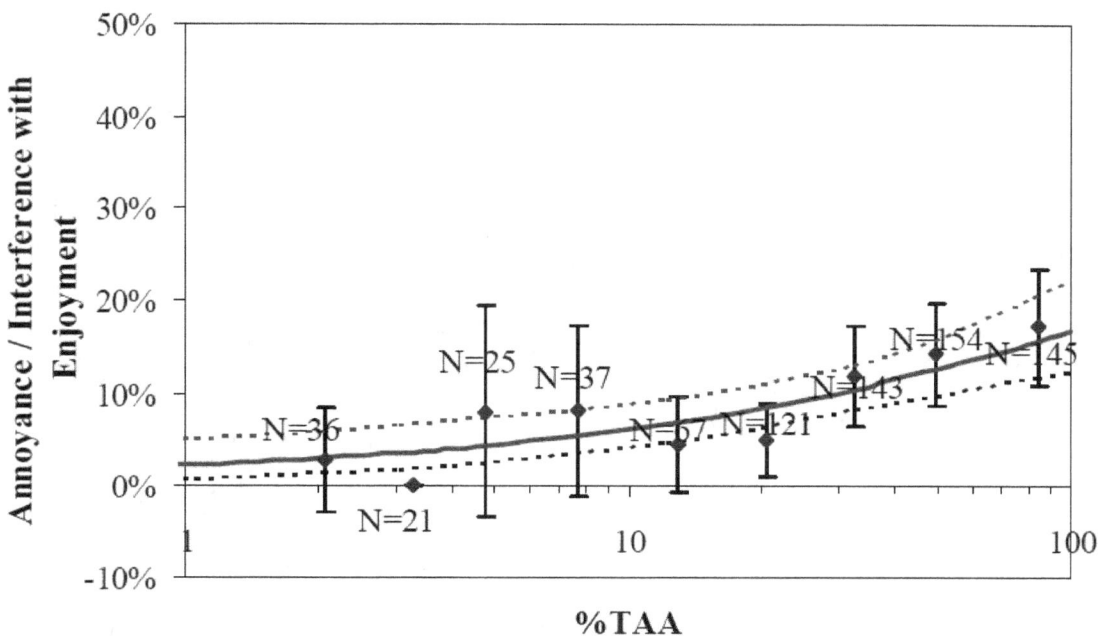

Figure G-19. Grouped Confidence Intervals vs. Regression Confidence Intervals, Overlooks, %TAA

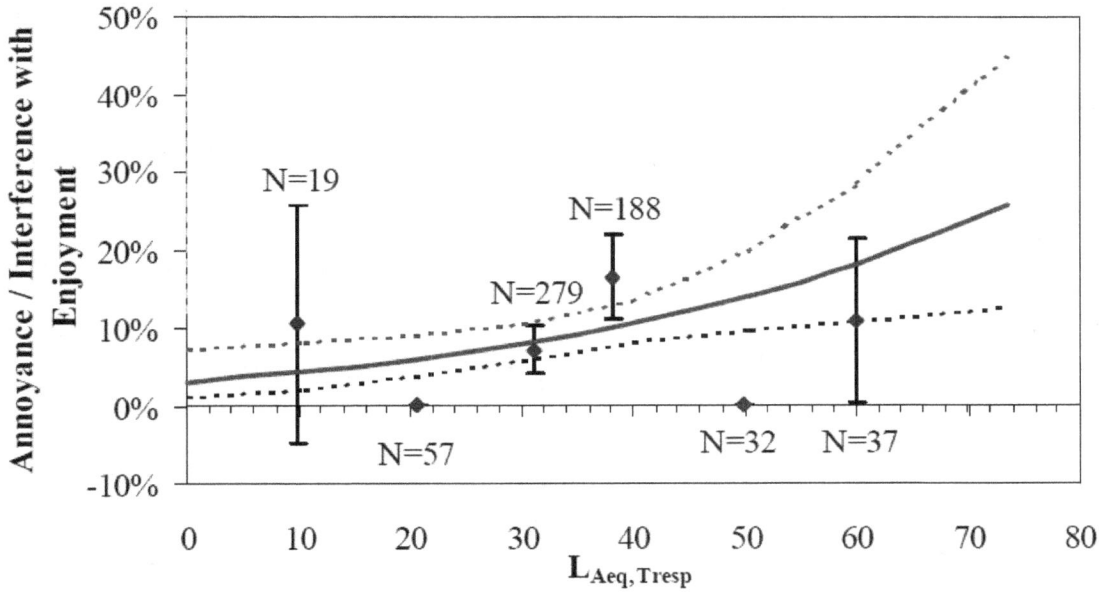

Figure G-20. Grouped Confidence Intervals vs. Regression Confidence Intervals, Overlooks, $L_{Aeq,Tresp}$

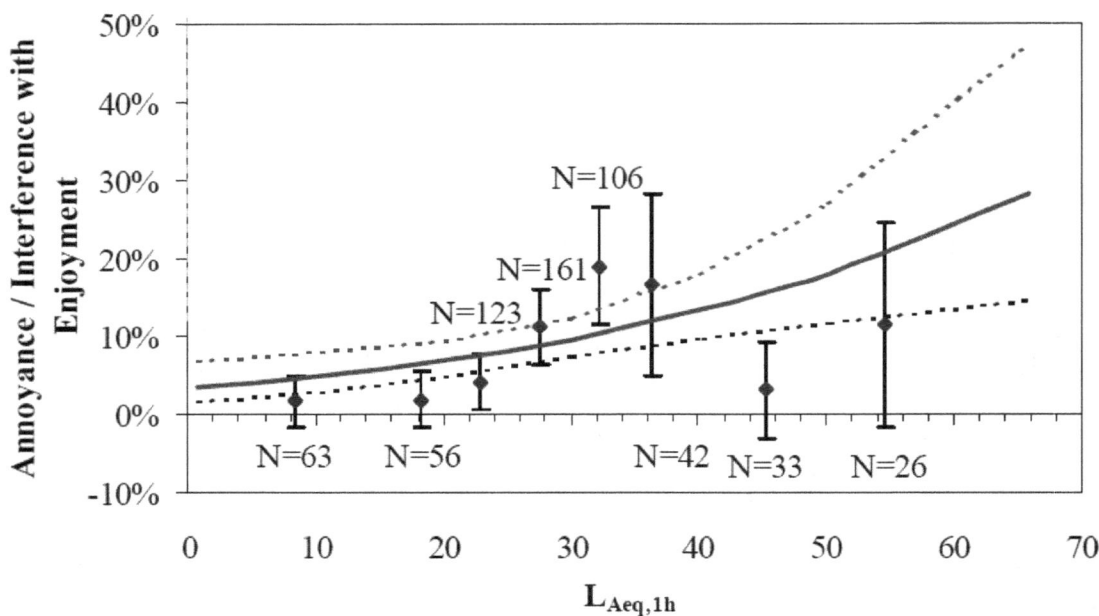

Figure G-21. Grouped Confidence Intervals vs. Regression Confidence Intervals, Overlooks, $L_{Aeq,1h}$

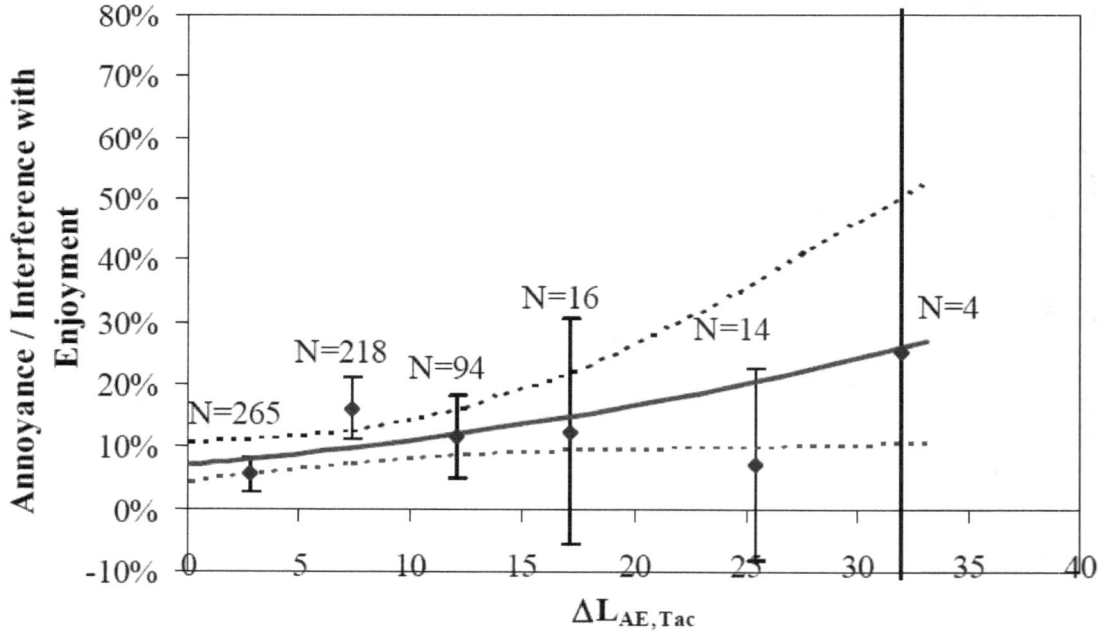

Figure G-22. Grouped Confidence Intervals vs. Regression Confidence Intervals, Overlooks, $\Delta L_{AE,Tac}$

Environmental Measurement and Modeling Division
Volpe Center Acoustics Facility
Study of Visitor Response to Air Tour and Other Aircraft Noise in National Parks

January 2005

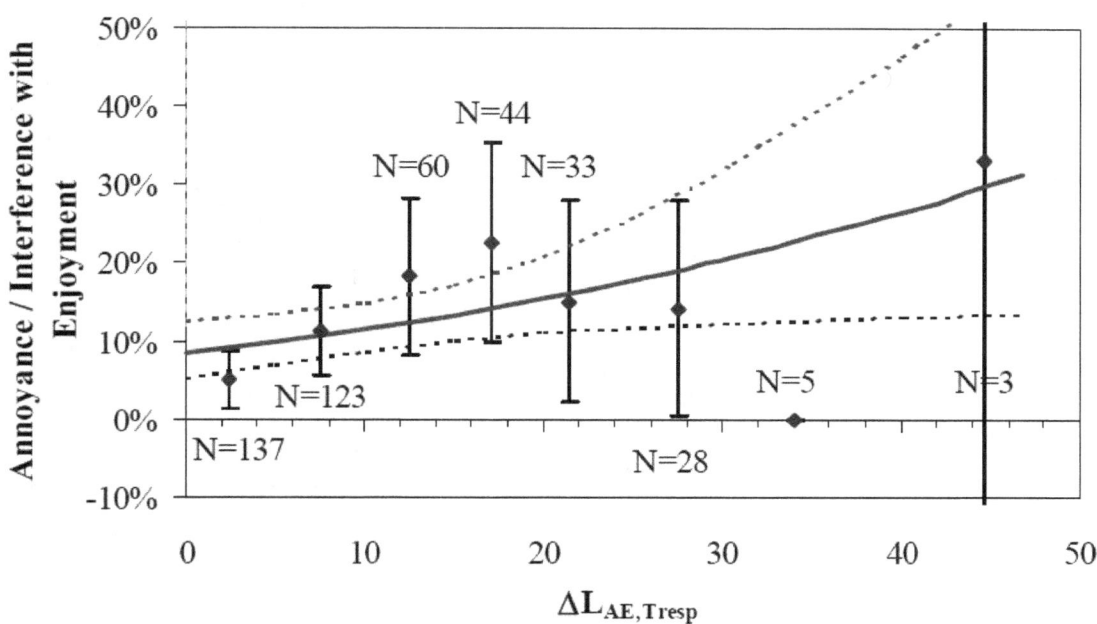

Figure G-23. Grouped Confidence Intervals vs. Regression Confidence Intervals, Overlooks, $\Delta L_{AE,Tresp}$

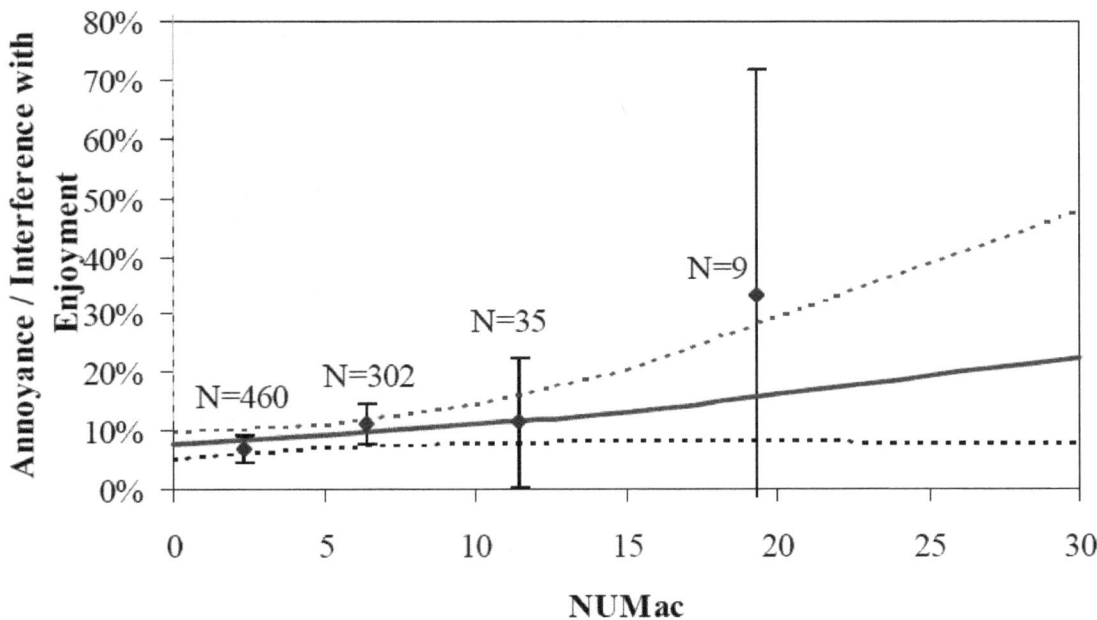

Figure G-24. Grouped Confidence Intervals vs. Regression Confidence Intervals, Overlooks, NUMac

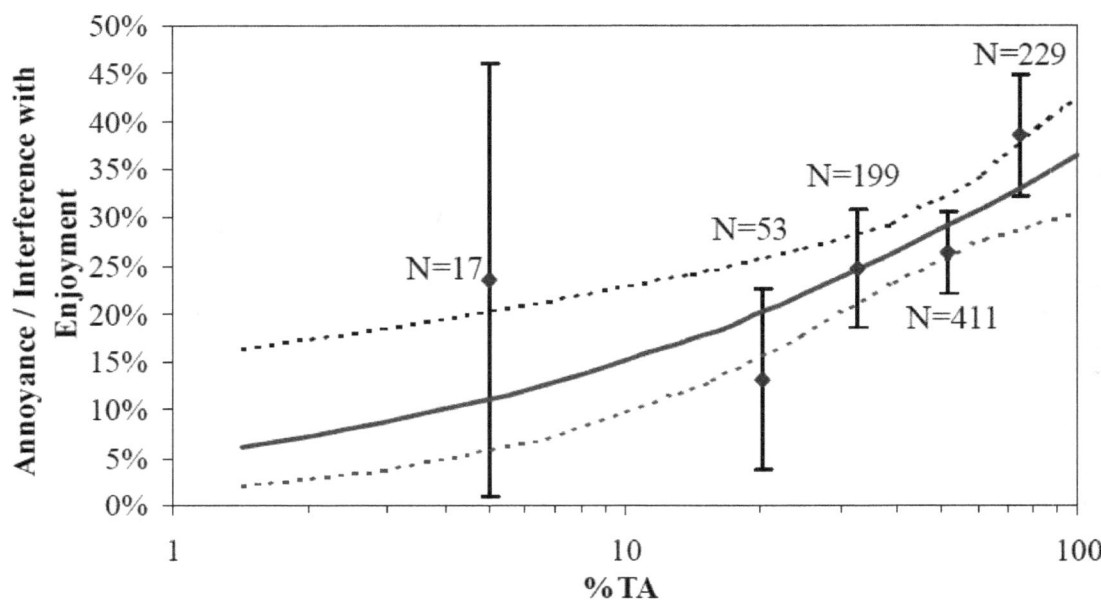

Figure G-25. Grouped Confidence Intervals vs. Regression Confidence Intervals, Short Hikes, %TA

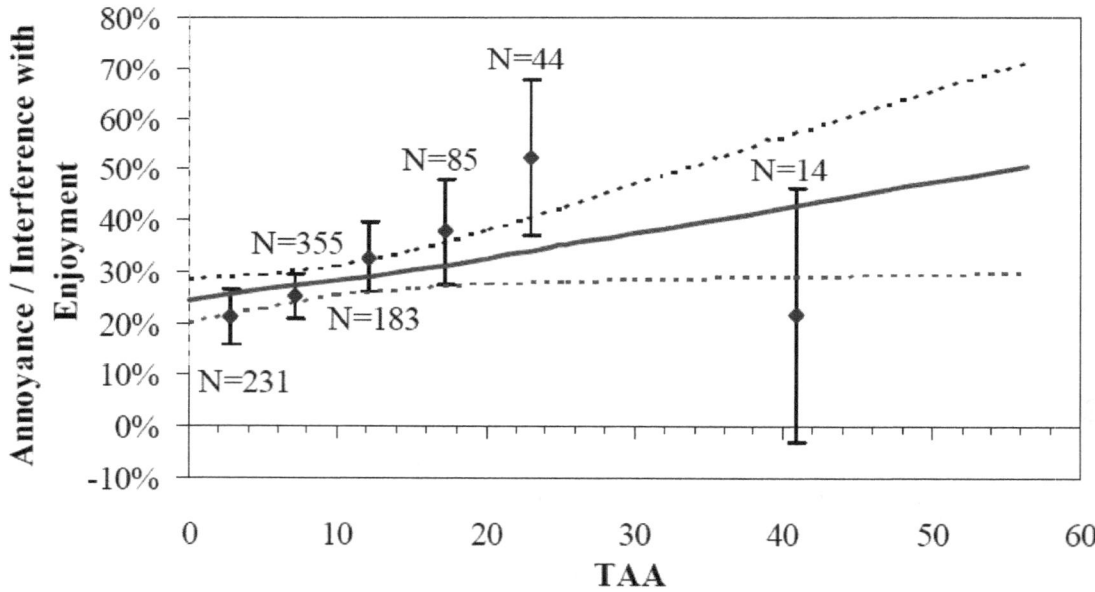

Figure G-26. Grouped Confidence Intervals vs. Regression Confidence Intervals, Short Hikes, TAA

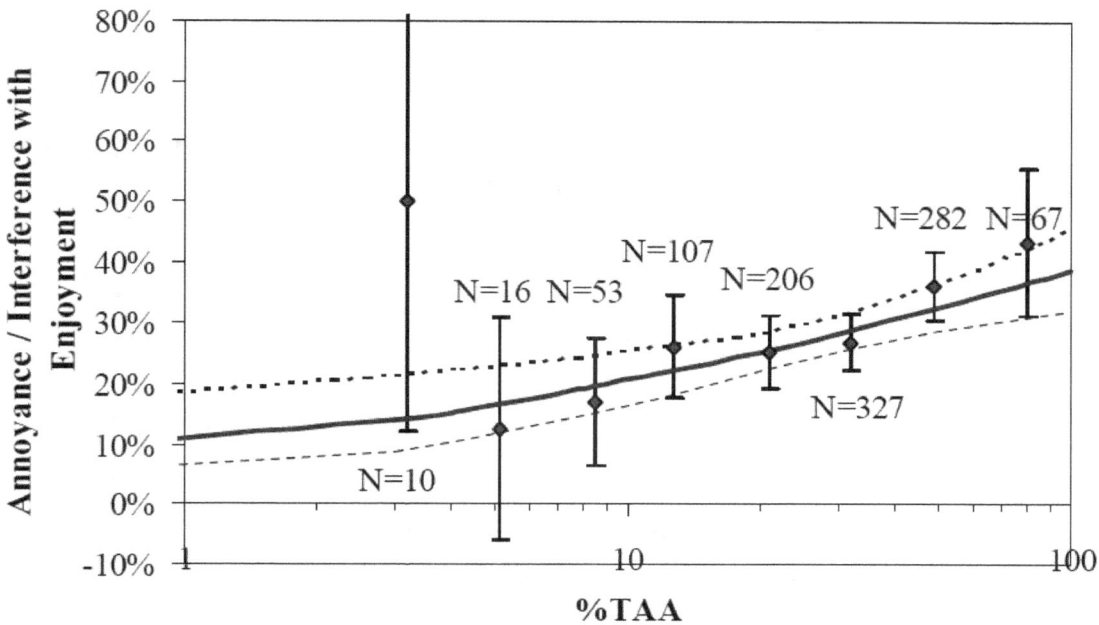

Figure G-27. Grouped Confidence Intervals vs. Regression Confidence Intervals, Short Hikes, %TAA

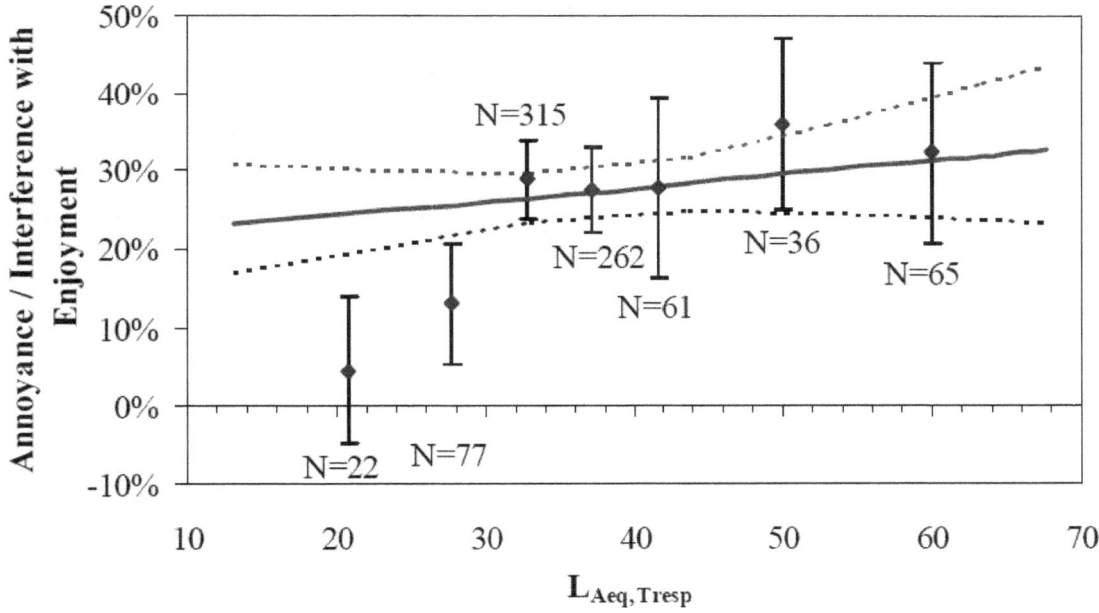

Figure G-28. Grouped Confidence Intervals vs. Regression Confidence Intervals, Short Hikes, $L_{Aeq,Tresp}$

Environmental Measurement and Modeling Division
Volpe Center Acoustics Facility
Study of Visitor Response to Air Tour and Other Aircraft Noise in National Parks

January 2005

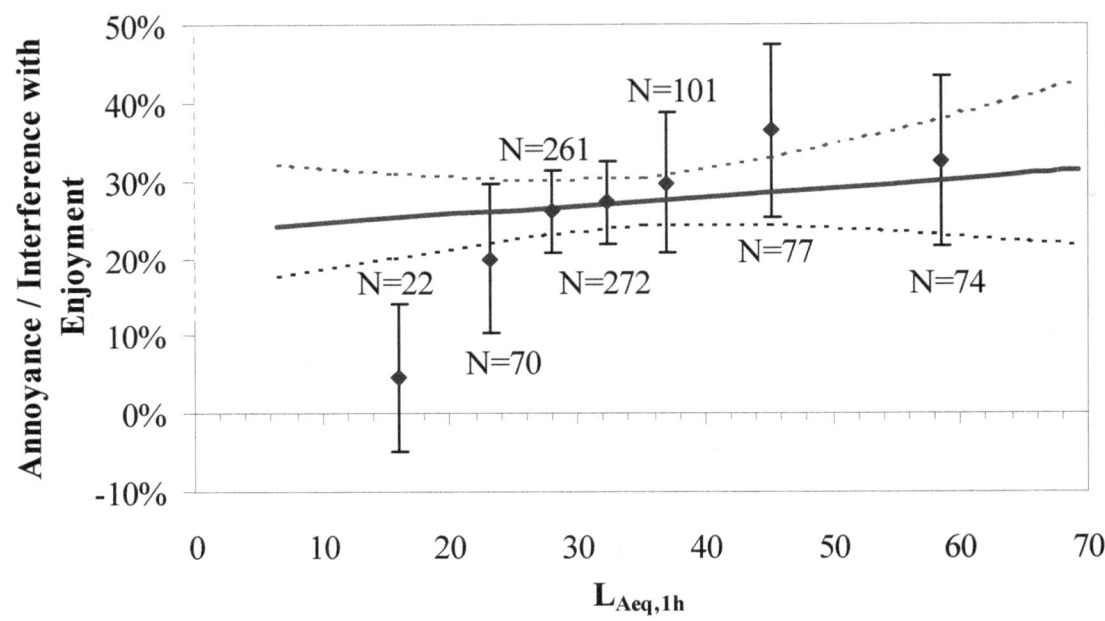

Figure G-29. Grouped Confidence Intervals vs. Regression Confidence Intervals, Short Hikes, $L_{Aeq,1h}$

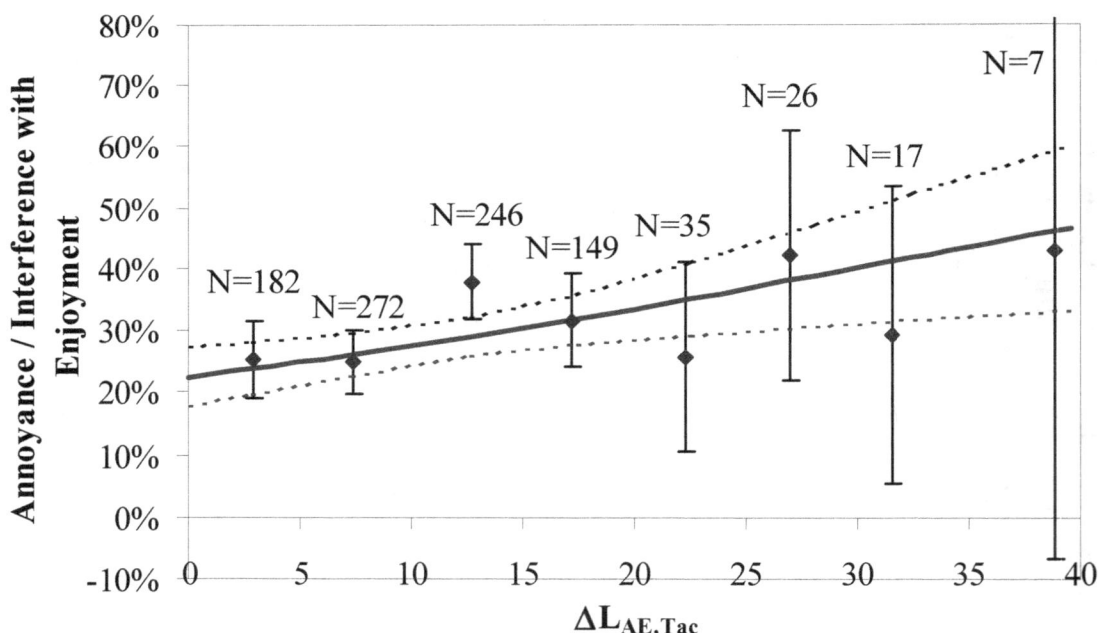

Figure G-30. Grouped Confidence Intervals vs. Regression Confidence Intervals, Short Hikes, $\Delta L_{AE,Tac}$

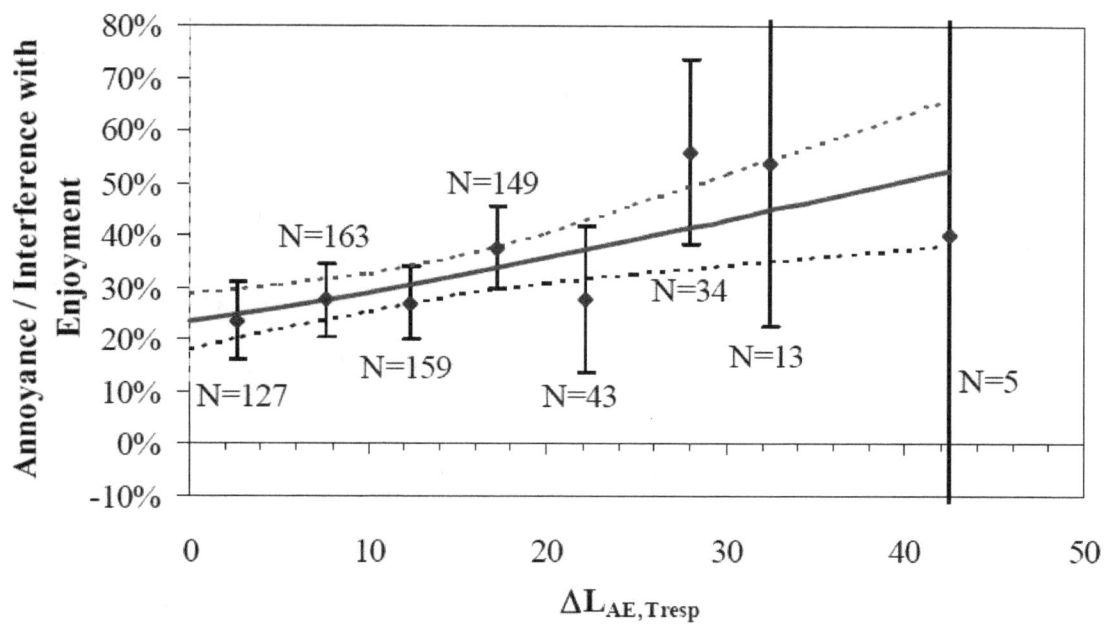

Figure G-31. Grouped Confidence Intervals vs. Regression Confidence Intervals, Short Hikes, $\Delta L_{AE,Tresp}$

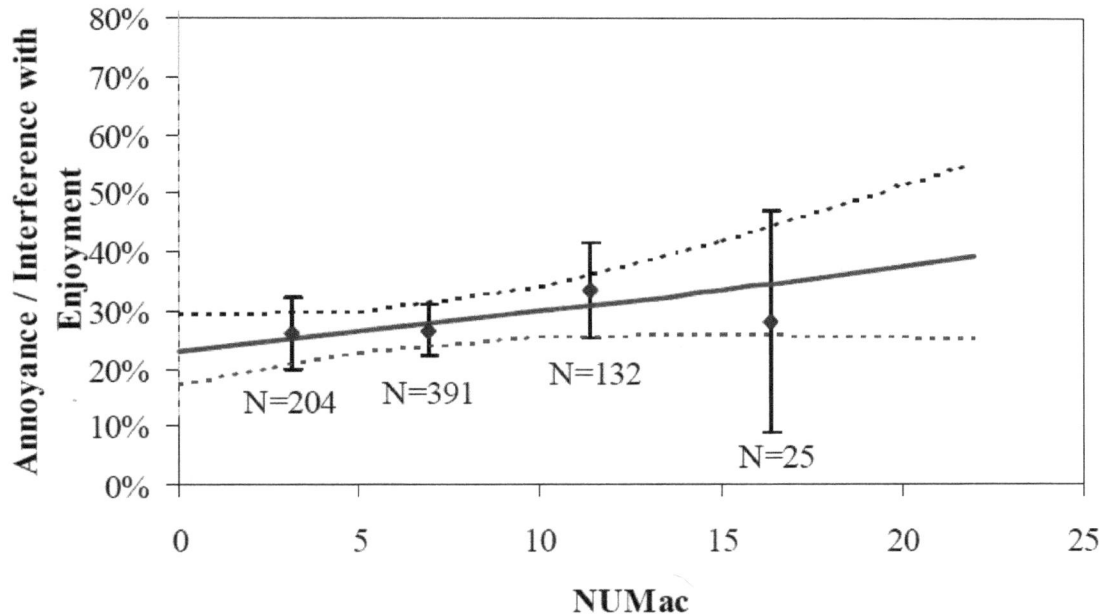

Figure G-32. Grouped Confidence Intervals vs. Regression Confidence Intervals, Short Hikes, NUMac